George John Youghusband

On Short Leave to Japan

George John Youghusband

On Short Leave to Japan

ISBN/EAN: 9783337166779

Printed in Europe, USA, Canada, Australia, Japan

Cover: Foto ©Andreas Hilbeck / pixelio.de

More available books at **www.hansebooks.com**

TEA-HOUSE WAITRESS

ON SHORT LEAVE TO JAPAN

BY
CAPTAIN G. J. YOUNGHUSBAND
QUEEN'S OWN CORPS OF GUIDES
AUTHOR OF 'EIGHTEEN HUNDRED MILES ON A
BURMESE TAT,' 'FRAYS AND FORAYS'
'THE QUEEN'S COMMISSION'

LONDON
SAMPSON LOW, MARSTON & COMPANY
Limited
St. Dunstan's House
FETTER LANE, FLEET STREET, E.C.
1894

PREFACE

I FEEL that it requires some hardihood to inflict on readers of travels yet another book on Japan. May my apology be that perchance the latest news of so interesting a country may not be altogether unacceptable to English readers? The following pages describe the unsophisticated wanderings of two young people through Japan during a few months' leave, taken from India. Perhaps it would not be too presumptuous to hope that those who know not the country will enjoy their trip on paper proportionately as much as we did ours on land; whilst those who have been in Japan, and know far more about it than we do, will, we trust, overlook such inaccuracies and fallacies as must necessarily occur in the work of a stray traveller in a strange land.

G. J. Y.

CONTENTS

CHAPTER I

PAGE

The length of India by train in the hot season—Calcutta—
A cyclone in Diamond Harbour—Storm-bound for four
days—Wrecks around us—The story of the *Namoa*—
The captain's yarns—His poor horse and its tragic end,   1

CHAPTER II

Penang—The Dutch war in Acheen—A fifty-year campaign—Enforced visit to the waterfall—'The Burmese Tat' again—Great preponderance of Chinamen—The way he is kept in order—The market—And its contents—The outer atmosphere of the 'dorian'—A Chinese wedding procession—Ingenious fishery, . . . 14

CHAPTER III

Singapore — Raffles — And Raffles Hotel — Temperature — Hosts of Celestials—The defences of Singapore—A first-class coaling station—An old coaling story—The astute Muscovite—The defences a form of national insurance against mercantile loss—Tanglin barracks and park—A commander-in-chief of one regiment—Our Jehu—The ponies—A lady in native costume at breakfast—Rickshaws—My Celestial tailor—Some notes about Chinamen—Opium — Exaggerating the evil—A blood-curdling sermon—'Bigotry, ignorance, and the hand of the Rev. Stiggins'—Chopsticks—Smoking tobacco—And opium

	PAGE
—Accident to machinery—A thirty-mile labyrinth of islands—Hong Kong, the Naples of the East—The head-steward—A princely income, ...	22

CHAPTER IV

Hong Kong—Excellent hotel—The racecourse—The Chinese pony—Polo—Sikh police—Some signboards—A cable-tram—The steepest railway on earth—The Peak—The garrison—The fleet—Chinese servants—Shops—Manilla cigars—The Messageries Maritimes—English the language of the world—Voyage to Shanghai—Shanghai—China Town—A Japanese lady—Her admirers—The Kassiwari—Caught in a fog—A dangerous day—Napkins and towels—Charging a cliff—JAPAN, . . . 38

CHAPTER V

The Inland Sea—Narrow passages—A sea train—Cold and rain in June—Kobé—Our first acquaintance with the man of Japan—His consuming politeness—The streets by night—The most effective time—A guard of honour—Chinese politeness—The shops of Kobé—Hiogo—The elevated river—To Yokohama by sea—Grand view of Mount Fuji, 12,450 feet high—Yokohama—Invaluable Murray—'Old Japan'—Temperature—Passports, . 58

CHAPTER VI

Sir Edwin Arnold and Mr. Clement Scott—Severe criticism of the Japanese women—A maledictory ode—Mr. Mitford's judicious words—Tokyo—Modern Japan—The Mikado of our imaginings—The Mikado as he is—Clipped daimios and modern Counts—Progress and other people's clothes—A Japanese lady in European clothes—An English lady in Japanese clothes—Substantial signs of civilisation—Telegraphs, posts, electric light, tramways, bicycles, hotels, police—Asakusa—The god with the bib—A short, sharp burst through 6771 volumes, . 69

CHAPTER VII

The Theatre—The Irving of Japan—A lengthy performance—The seating—Stage management—Sepulchral supers—The chorus—Refreshments—The plot of the play—*Hari-kiri*, the Japanese suicide—An account from *Old Japan*, ... 82

CHAPTER VIII

Tokyo by night—Holiday resorts—Our old friends 'the forty-seven'—Their pathetic story—The Shiba temples—The tombs of the Shoguns—Japan the Ramsgate of America—Ueno Park—The Mikado's bullock-cart—Christian relics—'Trampling boards'—Irises—Colonel Fukushima and his reception, ... 100

CHAPTER IX

Nikko—The journey there—Japanese railways—A Japanese hotel—Hospitable welcome—Excellent living—Our handmaid—Business letters—The mausolea—Short history of Ieyasu, ... 110

CHAPTER X

The tomb of a great soldier—Described in detail—Rainiest place in Japan—'A chair that gets up with you'—Under strict discipline—Lake Chuzenji—Ponies—Round the world playing billiards—The slapdash tourist—The god 'Humbug'—The goddess 'Jingo'—Fur slippers—Nikko scenery, ... 119

CHAPTER XI

Hot springs in the hills—Ikao—A tedious journey—A courteous stationmaster—Some hotels deteriorate—The reason why—Luxurious hot baths—Natural dyeing properties—Lake Haruna—Our cab-horse—Harrowing stories—Indiscreet paper walls—Their advantages—Educating the toes—A cheap resort, ... 137

CHAPTER XII

Telegrams—Postage—By train—First class or second class?—Japanese fellow-travellers—A first-class hotel—Train, tram, and rickshaw to Mujanoshita—Disappointed with it—A *bento* box—Hakoné Lake—In Japan again—'Hell's caldron'—Adam and Eve again—Why not?—Missionaries and missionaries—Foster-mothers—Philandering—Fishing—'Ye banks and braes o' bonnie Doon'—Away, away—A *kago*, ... 146

CHAPTER XIII

The aboriginal inn—The Tokaido—Magnificent views—Sandals for man and beast—The rickshaw man, and some reflections on him—A village tea-house—Japanese gardens—Our way of living—An embarrassing bath—Luxurious beds—On to Lake Biwa—Inhospitality—The old daimio's castle—By steamer to Otsu—The 'assassination' of the Czarewitch, ... 158

CHAPTER XIV

The ancient capital—Mr Clement Scott again—Some reflections by an onlooker—'Prison-editors'—The Mikado of old—Kyoto *v.* Tokyo—The Abacus—Japanned English—The purchasing mania—The town at night—The Mikado's palace—A boy engineer, . 174

CHAPTER XV

Osaka—Dante's *Inferno*—The river by night—Nara—The Daibutsu—A mermaid—The waters of Takaradzuka—'Sayona,' 192

CHAPTER XVI

Financial—Expenses of journey to Japan—Curio buying—Hotels in India, China, and Japan—Town hotels in Japan—Hill hotels—Country inns—' Tips '—' The pestilential guide '—Through the Customs—Money—Spring, summer, autumn, or winter?—With an unbiassed mind, . 197

CHAPTER XVII

The army of Japan—The death of feudalism—Rise of the standing army—Japan's instructors—Strength—Conscription—Pay—Uniform—Physique—Martial spirit—Barracks—Rations—The officers—Their messes—The infantry: armament: drill—Cavalry: horses: armament: strength of units: stables: fodder: saddle—Artillery—A political factor in the East—*V.* China—With Siam—Press power—And how it may be used, . 210

LIST OF ILLUSTRATIONS

		PAGE
PLEASE OBSERVE THE NAILS, ...	*To face*	46
TEA-HOUSE WAITRESS, ...	,,	71
A SAMURAI (THE FIGHTING CLASS), . . .	,,	116
THE TOMB OF A GREAT SOLDIER, . . .	,,	119
PREPARING THE BATH, ...	,,	128
OUR HOTEL AT HAKONÉ, ...	,,	150
JAPANESE LADY IN CHAIR, ...	,,	158
CALCULATING MACHINE, ...	,,	179

CHAPTER I

A STORMY START

By a curious fatality, we chose, or rather the fates chose for us, probably the worst week in the year for our start. That week commenced on May 19th. Up to that date it had been remarkably cool in our part of the world, and frequent mention was made in the papers of an equally satisfactory state of affairs the whole way down the line. However, the moment we stepped on board the train, all that was altered. The thermometer ran up to 102° that day, 107° the second day, and a trifle higher the third day. Our journey lay the whole length of India from the vicinity of Peshawur to Calcutta, and occupied three days and three nights; so we were more than glad when we could look back on it, as part of a disagreeable past, from the cool and airy rooms of the Great Eastern Hotel.

Calcutta was quite at its best: it was not too hot, and certainly not too cold; not too wet, but just wet enough. The change from the harsh, dry heat of 'up country' was very soothing, and made itself apparent in the unlimited capacity for sleep which was suddenly developed.

Whilst I was down at the Pay Office, having my accounts settled up, two large black balls flew up to a neighbouring mast-head. 'That means bad weather,' said the clerk; 'and if a drum is hoisted instead, it means a cyclone.' Next day the balls were still up, but we made a start; though by the time Diamond Harbour, some forty miles down the river, was reached, the wind came on to blow a perfect hurricane. The cyclone was upon us. The *Catherine Apcar* was immediately anchored, the awning taken down, and everything made fast for a furious night. Heavens, how it blew! The registered rate of the wind was about a hundred miles an hour. I should have said, roughly speaking, that it was at least a thousand. That is where fact and fiction clash together in

A STORMY START

such an inconsiderate manner — for the fiction.

My recollection of the cyclone was as follows:—The wind blew at the rate of a thousand miles an hour; the sea rose mountains high. The upper deck was crowded with sheep and goats, bullocks and horses; but the wind thought nothing of these. At first the sheep and goats, and, as it gained strength, the horses and bullocks, were whisked into the air like straws by a dust-devil. The captain was blown clean through the wheel-house, leaving a round hole like a cannon-shot; and all the deck passengers were turned into quava jelly mixed with salt water. The saloon passengers, clothed only in life-belts, sat mournfully each on his little pile of luggage, and wished they were anywhere else in the world. The captain's three dogs were blown out of their skins, and these latter hang in the saloon as a silent record of the sad fact. The pilot used language fit for a bishop, and drank whisky cocktails with a quiet persistency which left nothing to be desired; and so on, and so on : something like a storm indeed. But the uncompromising counterbalance of fact brings us down to the reality—and that was sad enough.

It had been blowing hard— very hard, a landsman would say—all night ; but at 6 A.M. on the 25th the cyclone caught us. In a storm, what sailors like is sea-room ; this is well known. Our feelings, therefore, may be imagined when, on looking out of a port-hole, it was apparent that to throw a biscuit on shore would have been quite an easy feat. Further inquiry showed that we were steaming full speed ahead, and had already paid out two hundred fathoms (nearly a quarter of a mile) of cable since casting anchor. Breakfast that morning was not as cheerful a meal as usual, and in the middle of it the pilot came down to say that a large ship had just gone booming past to certain destruction. At this moment some one looking out of window exclaimed, 'There's a sand-bank quite close!' General adjournment to the window, and there, sure enough, between the waves appeared a rounded, slate-coloured object, which could be nothing but a sandbank. What was more, it was gradually growing nearer; in other words, we were drifting on to it. We all had an ugly few minutes, and then a sharp-eyed sailor discovered that it was the keel of a capsized vessel of some sort drifting across our stern. Universal thanksgiving, and more breakfast. A cyclone generally lasts for twelve hours or so, and then moves off elsewhere; or rather it is moving all the time, thus—

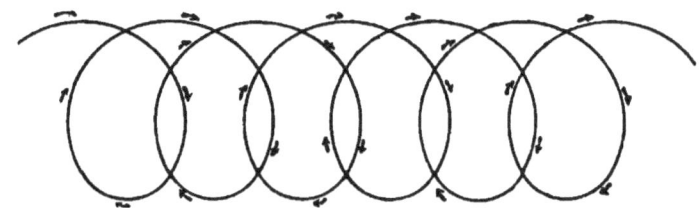

round and round, and yet drifting all the time. Our cyclone, however, lasted three days and three nights, with pouring, driving rain the whole time.

During these days we had no news from shore, and only learnt later the full extent of the damage done. But from before our eyes disappeared one large steamer into the driving mist and her doom beyond; and on the shore close by appeared one morning a huge four-masted sailing-ship, bow first, high and dry, but standing almost upright, and to an inexperienced eye little damaged. This was the *William Tell*, the captain told us—one of those unlucky ships which is always getting into trouble. She was comparatively new, but had started badly. During her trial trip in the English Channel, she rolled so badly that the crew, being convinced that she would capsize, deserted her, and she was abandoned to her fate. But, later, a pilot-boat came across her, and the men, boarding the deserted vessel, brought her safely to harbour: and what was more, claimed salvage, and got it! She has probably done her last voyage now, anyhow.

As we put to sea on the third day, we passed a sunken steamer, the *Anglia*, and afterwards heard the ghastly story of her loss. It appears that she touched a sand-bank, heeled over, and capsized in the course of a few seconds; but the water she fell over in was not very deep at that moment, and one side of her remained above water. The majority of the passengers and crew got off in boats or on floating spars; but a few were caught below in their cabins. We have often read of martyrs of old who were tied to posts in the sea, and left to drown by inches with the rising tide. Imagine, then, the fate of these poor fellows. The port-holes were just large enough for a man to put his head through, but no more. The ship was of iron, and to enlarge the holes in the time available was an impossibility, though an endeavour was made with cold chisels. The boats from another ship came alongside, and handed food and drink to the doomed men, and gave them such encouragement as was possible. But the tide rose inch by inch, and at last the time arrived when it seemed better for all that the boats should leave; for to remain was but to prolong the agony on both sides. Some of the imprisoned cursed and foamed at the mouth with anguish, some prayed, some in the cold sweat of despair beseeched the boats' crews to shoot them ere they went. Sadly and silently the boats slipped away; the tide rose, and the last shrieks of the dying men sank into the sigh of the rising waves. One feels tempted to ask, Why were men created to die in such awful agony? A villain commits a cold-blooded and atrocious murder, and he is relieved of life by the law as comfortably as is consistent with circumstances. On the other hand, an innocent and blameless man goes to sea for pleasure or business, and he is put to death with the profoundest form of cruelty. Strange problems, these!

Looking round the saloon, two cases of Martini-Henry rifles, with sword-bayonets, and a dozen revolvers were noticeable. These are carried as a precautionary measure against such a seizure as befel the *Namoa* a year or two ago in the China seas. A large band of Chinese pirates, disguised as peaceful deck-passengers, came on board at Amoa. One night, a few days from land, whilst the ship officers and passengers were at dinner, the ship was systematically seized.

One party of Chinamen overpowered the officer on watch and the man at the wheel; another party seized the whole of the engineers and stokers; whilst a third party surrounded the saloon, and deliberately shot down the captain and such of the officers and passengers as they could catch sight of. The pirates now completely looted the ship, placing all the specie and valuables in boats; they then disabled the engines and steering-gear, and rowed off, leaving the ship to her fate. Fortunately, the surviving officers were able to patch up the engines and the steering-gear sufficiently to enable the ship with much difficulty to struggle on to Hong Kong. Of course, a strong protest was lodged with the Chinese Government, and reparation demanded. As with all Asiatic Powers, procrastination was the first diplomatic weapon employed. But the brutal British Government is very blunt in its dealings with second-rate Powers; and visions of gunboats and redcoats began to loom before the eyes of the King of Heaven and his advisers. In polite deference, therefore, to this barbaric pressure from without, thirty-two Chinese pirates were executed, and the execution commemorated by instantaneous photographs. Perhaps it would be taking too hopeful a view of Chinese enlightenment to trust that these thirty-two men were the true culprits. In the annals of photography, possibly nothing equals the appalling hideousness of this scene.

A heavy swell and a smart south-westerly gale met us as we put to sea; and life on board the pilot-brig, here anchored, looked most uncomfortable. One lightship had disappeared altogether, and we heard later had been lost with all hands; and the other was being towed into her place again as we passed. It is impossible to imagine how any one can be persuaded to live on a lightship, or for the matter of that on a pilot-brig, for any salary under £2000 per annum. The sea has absolutely no charms for me when it is rough, and therefore I thank heaven fervently that fate did not make me a sailor. She very nearly did, though;

for, being much enamoured of Marryat's novels and hating Greek Grammar, one of the masters at school was privately induced by me to coach me for the navy. When my preparations were complete and I was considered ready to pass the examination, I sprang my intentions suddenly on my father. As far as I remember, the tightest part of my trousers was severely corrected, and I was sent clattering back to school. For which small mercy I have never yet ceased to be thankful, and the navy is to be congratulated on the loss of a bad bargain. The conversation turned at dinner on the strength and variety of objurgations as a vehicle for expressing one's feelings. The captain capped the collection. He was riding on top of a 'bus which ran down a milk-barrow. A wild torrent of choice expletives was naturally expected from the barrow, and the passengers, missing it, looked over to see if it was coming. They saw a man with a bright purple face, bursting with rage, but temporarily dumb. At last the volcano broke, and out came, 'Well, there ain't no word for it!!'

A couple of days of severe pitching and tumbling brought us under the lee of the Andaman Islands, and into smooth water. A bright sky overhead and a light headwind combined to make the weather perfect. One of the passengers was heard to remark that he always felt born to be an admiral on these sort of days; so do most of us. A horse was on board for Singapore, and the change to smooth water did not seem to suit him, for he fell ill at once. With the aid of the *Sea Captain's Medical Guide* and the ship's medicine-box, we all had a turn at that poor horse. The captain was a great believer in castor-oil for all illness; he looked up the doses for an able seaman, and doubled them for his horse. When the castor-oil keg ran dry, I had my turn with sweet spirits of nitre; and when that ran dry, a medical practitioner amongst the passengers tried a few fancy pills. Meanwhile, three or four native horse-dealers dovetailed in their remedies; the least drastic being a mixture of burnt cocoanut matting and water given by the bucketful.

They also squirted goat's milk up his nostrils, and smeared his nose with sheep's droppings. Curiously enough, this compendium of remedies did not kill him outright. He was a hardy horse, and survived the treatment three days.

On the fifth day out we fetched Penang harbour, the weather still being perfect and the sea quite smooth.

CHAPTER II

A HARBOUR IN THE TROPICS

PENANG is a snug, clean little place buried in the most extravagant form of tropical verdure. Little ferns and plants which in England we see struggling along in six-inch pots in carefully kept hothouses, here reach the size of trees. The rarest and most delicate orchids grow in the wildest profusion, with nothing but trellis-work to protect them from the weather. Fruit of every tropical kind thrives and flourishes in the rich soil and moist, temperate heat. The climate varies little all the year round, and it is possible, if not always actually pleasant, to be out and about all day. The fierce heat which in summer closes our doors for eight hours a day in Upper India is unknown.

In the harbour we found a Dutch man-of-war, up from Acheen, laying in stores.

Acheen lies at the north corner of Sumatra, and has furnished the Dutch army and navy with a little pocket-campaign which has lasted now, they tell me, for nearly twenty-five years. The people of Penang have become quite callous about this war; and when a Dutch war-vessel dashes in for stores and dashes off again, as if for a second battle of Trafalgar, they only smile and pocket their dollars. We saw several brave Dutchmen with strings of medals on. These are gathered in the happy hunting-ground of Acheen. However, the Dutch are not the only people who

> 'Gather medals all the day,
> And wear them all the night;'

for I remember an officer at Rawul-Pindi, who had never left Rawul-Pindi during the year 1882, being summarily decorated with a silver medal, a bronze star, and the Order of the Osmanieh, as a reward for his services during the Egyptian Campaign of 1882![1]

[1] This officer, of course, returned the medals to the authorities; but his name appeared amongst those 'mentioned in despatches' in that campaign!

At Penang, of course, we made the usual pilgrimage to the botanical gardens and the waterfall. The gardens are very neat, and beautifully arranged; but the waterfall was not working up to full power. Whether one wants to or not, it is impossible to avoid visiting these two places of interest, for the local Jehu carries a stranger straight there, *nolens volens.* When we landed, my first desire in life was to buy some collars, and I directed the driver to go to a collar-shop. 'Very good, sah,' and off he dashed to the waterfall, which is four miles away, and at least three and a half miles, as the crow flies, from the nearest collar. One of our fellow-passengers, an officer on inspection duty, arrayed in uniform, also entered a hired carriage, and, pointing to his helmet and sword, said 'Barracks!' several times over. 'Very good, sah,' and off he went to the waterfall.

Next morning we landed again, and stepped into a carriage without saying a word: nor did the driver, but just whipped round his pony and started off for the falls.

But we knew the ways of the place well now, and pulled him up 'all standing,' and made him take us a tour of the bazaar and native thoroughfares. We met here again our old friend the Burmese tat, or pony. He stands about twelve hands two inches high, and is a perfect little horse in miniature. It is really a wonderful sight to see the little fellow rattling along a four-wheeled vehicle with four fat Chinamen inside and a thin driver on the box-seat. Even with this load behind him it is no uncommon thing to see him trot past a fifteen-hand Australian horse, harnessed to a similar vehicle. If the Burmah pony were six inches higher, and still retained his present qualities, he would be the wonder of the world.

The most striking feature of the Penang thoroughfares is the vast proportion of Chinamen that throng the streets and decorate every shop-door. I have no statistics by me, but the proportion of Chinamen to the rest of the population must be ten to one. These are kept in order in two ways. The first is a physical agency in the shape of a detachment of British infantry, and Sikh police. The second is a moral influence, which takes the curious form of a threat that if a Chinaman makes a nuisance of himself he will be at once deported to China. Perhaps the reception he receives there makes him averse to this forcible visit to his paternal acres; for the moment he lands he is seized by the pigtail and there and then beheaded. For the Emperor of China says, 'If this man is such a bad character that they can't keep him at Penang or Singapore, I'm certainly not going to have him let loose in China, so " off with his head;"' and off it is.

The Penang market is a clean, wholesome, and orderly place; indeed, the whole municipal management must be excellent. The state of the roads, the excellent sanitation, and the generally clean look of the whole place, give an air of prosperity not to be found in most Indian cantonments, with their dilapidated mud-walls and oceanic compounds.[1] Fish and fruit are abundant

---

[1] The space round an Indian house; sometimes made into a garden, as often left desolate.

and good; the latter comprising mangoes, mangosteens, dorian, and plantains. The mangosteen is considered by epicures to be superior to the mango. Perhaps it is; but as the two fruits are as different from one another as gooseberries from pears, it is difficult to form an opinion. They say that the dorian is the most delicious fruit to be found in the East. We have had to take this statement on trust, for so far no one on board has managed to get within a cable's length of one. The smell of them is only to be compared to that which emanates from large sewage-works. Once you cut your way through this outer atmosphere, the fruit is said to be excellent in taste.

There are a few European shops scattered through the bazaar, a sprinkling of Indian tradesmen struggle along; but the vastly preponderating trading influence is that of the ubiquitous Celestial. In one street we passed a Chinese marriage feast being borne along in procession. First came piles of sweets made in huge star-shaped platters; next, rows of large fish just caught; then a whole scalded pig, followed by a goat on another tray. Besides eatables, one litter must have contained at least a hundred pairs of highly ornamented shoes, whilst another contained two or three dozens of brandy, beer, etc. A closed hired carriage, over which was held a huge state umbrella, led the way.

The energetic fishermen amongst the residents have discovered a unique and effective way of baiting their fishing-grounds. First an immense cylindrical basket, as large as a good-sized room, and made of open bamboo-work, is constructed. This structure, heavily weighted, is sunk at some favourable spot in the sea, and the place marked by a buoy. Nature does the rest in the course of six months or so. Gradually seaweed, limpets, and odds-and-ends of submarine animalculæ, settle on to the basket, and by degrees cover it completely. Next comes a colony of little fishes, which live, and fatten, and increase on the excellent diets afforded by the limpets, etc. Having waxed fat and grown delicious-looking, large fish find this a happy hunting-ground for the appeasement of their appetites, and visit it regularly to eat the little fish. Finally, the original and rightful owner of the large basket, the fisherman, comes along and catches the big fish, and eats *him*. A submarine tragedy in three acts; with the whole company, in a condensed form, assisting at the theatrical supper afterwards.

Two more bright days, with the sea like glass, brought us by way of the Straits of Malacca to Singapore. So far, exclusive of four days' detention owing to the cyclone, our voyage had occupied eight days, of which six and a half were at sea.

CHAPTER III

A FIRST-CLASS COALING STATION

SINGAPORE is quite near enough to the Equator to be termed on it. From the map of the world it appears that we lie here in the latitude of the Victoria Nyanza Lake in Africa and the mouth of the Amazon River in South America. There appears to be only one town in the world actually on the Equator, and that is Quito. Though Singapore is some 1500 miles south of Calcutta, it is doubtful whether it is so hot. On June 6th, one of the hottest days in the year, the thermometer registered only 84° at Singapore. To such salamanders as we become in Upper India, this seems quite temperate; but, as a matter of fact, 84° of damp heat is equivalent to over 90° of dry heat. In Singapore it is not impossible to be out and about all day, and doors and windows remain open night and day.

We decided to live on shore, and were recommended to Raffles Hotel. In my unpardonable ignorance I inquired whether Raffles was an Englishman, and whether he managed the hotel himself, or intrusted it to a manager. This was rather an unhappy question, for to my confusion it appeared that Raffles was the name of the great man who raised the colony. On further acquaintance we found his name emblazoned on his offspring: for besides the Hotel there were Raffles Museum, Raffles Boys' School, Raffles Girls' School, Raffles Plain, and Raffles Statue. Raffles Hotel was clean and comfortable, and the rooms large and airy. We enjoyed much the change from on board ship.

Again hosts of Chinamen, 120,000 in all, seemed to claim the town their own; for the sprinkling of Malays and Madrassis merely goes to emphasise the preponderance of the Heathen Chinee. This large foreign element is overawed physically by one British regiment of infantry and a handful of Sikh policemen: morally, as at Penang, with a threat of transportation to China—and the inevitable result. There are only about 1000 English residents. Against external foes Singapore is, they tell me, practically impregnable, by reason of its submarine mines and coast batteries, whilst a very nasty-looking fort completely sweeps the roadstead and anchorage. Of course, these works do not profess to block the straits—that is a naval matter—but merely to secure absolutely the coaling station. Coal seems a prosaic enough article, and it is hard to connect it, in imagination, with great deeds and great battles. But nothing impresses on one more forcibly the immense power of the British navy than the consummate skill with which its coaling stations are dotted over the world. It is no uncommon thing to hear our navy compared in numbers and strength to the navies of other nations. That seems to me to be a false estimate of comparative strength. For one big battle in the English Channel these statistics may hold good; but in the great war which our navy will wage all over the world, I submit that the combined navies of all Europe cannot stand against her for a moment, *as long as her coaling stations are secure.* In this connection an interesting fact came to light the other day. Until recently the Cape of Good Hope was not connected by telegraph with England, which gave an opening for the following clever stratagem on the part of Russia. One of the periodical war scares was then in full swing, and a collision between England and Russia seemed inevitable. A strict watch was kept on the Russian fleet, and to every one's surprise it went off on a seemingly aimless cruise to Monte Video, of all places in the world. But the cruise was far from aimless, for Monte Video is connected by telegraph with St. Petersburg, and is much nearer to the Cape of Good Hope than England is. A glance at the map of the world will demonstrate the strength of the position. The moment war was declared, the Russian fleet was to go full steam to St. Helena, burn all the coal there; then hurry off to the Cape again, burning all the coal; so on to Mauritius and Aden, at each place burning the coal. Pursuit without coal would be impossible, and without coal no merchantmen would reach England for months with the news. In conjunction with this scheme, of course, the Suez Canal was to be accidentally (?) blocked. If everything had come off successfully—and there was no great improbability in the matter—India and our Eastern trade would have been at the mercy of the Russian fleet for three or four months. But we have altered all that now, and could, not improbably, play the game of sea warfare successfully against the fleets of the world.

Kindly imagine, for instance, the desperate position of the French in Cochin China if war were declared to-morrow. Thousands of miles from France, with a fleet not half the strength of ours in these waters, not a coaling station except Saigon in the hemisphere, and their only telegraph line running to a British port.

These thoughts fill one with pride, and prevent one's sympathies siding with the people of Singapore, who are at present very angry at being obliged to pay for the necessary defensive works and the guns to man them. It seems to an outsider merely a form of insurance, for certainly without modern works and modern guns the Singapore merchant and his business would be in a very precarious position in time of war.

These warlike reflections were suggested by the current rumour, at the time of our visit, that the relations between France and England were much strained in reference to Siamese affairs.

Let us return to peaceful Singapore. We drove out to Tanglin barracks and the public gardens there. The former, unlike ordinary barracks, were very picturesque, and more especially so the officers' quarters and mess—deeply thatched, with cool broad verandahs, and buried in every sort of tropical vegetation. The gardens are beautifully kept, and are very lovely. On the way out to the gardens, which are three and a half miles from the town, we passed the governor's residence, a fine building standing on a commanding eminence and surrounded by a very

English-looking park. The governor is a civilian, and he is supported by a lieutenant-governor and commander-in-chief, at present Sir Charles Warren, late of the London police. The lieutenant-governor and commander-in-chief has one regiment, a couple of batteries, and a company of sappers in his command. The more one sees of the world, the more the conviction comes home that, in spite of its drawbacks, India is the only country worth soldiering in. Fancy, after a long and meritorious career, being sent to the ends of the world to command one regiment and a battery or two. Or, equally bad, to be put in command of three men and a boy on Southsea Common, and be expected to spend £2000 a year of private means in keeping up the dignity of the position.

Our driver was a very intelligent and obliging Madrassi, full of information, and talking English well. He said, 'Not proper great lady and gentleman drive in hired carriage. I fetch good carriage for master,' which he accordingly did, bringing a private carriage—whose property, heaven knows!—and drove us about in great state. Moreover, he charged us nothing extra for the luxury. The best ponies, or indeed animals of any sort, come from Dêli up the coast; they are very much like Burmah ponies, and, if anything, a degree better. They fetch as much as 300 and 350 dollars,[1] and are priced on a par with imported Walers.

At breakfast at the hotel an elderly lady close to us very nearly had a fit, and certainly to English eyes the costume of another fair creature who had just entered was—well—very airy. She was a pretty woman, with hair done in the latest fashion, but the rest of her costume consisted of a linen jacket—bed-jacket, I believe, it is called—and a sarong or lungi round the loins, such as is worn by Burmese women. Her legs and feet were bare, and on the ends of her toes were balanced a pair of slippers. With her were a very correctly attired gentleman and a little boy. It appeared that they were Dutch people from Batavia, and in Batavia

[1] The dollar fluctuates, but is now worth 2s. 6d., or 2 Rs.

all the ladies wear native costumes till sundown, shopping, calling, and doing all their household business thus airily clad. The English lady before alluded to got so transfixed and purple with horror, that before the end of breakfast she looked as if she had fed on nothing but prawn curries for several years.

After dinner we went for a rickshaw ride. The rickshaws are rather broader than those in use in India, and perhaps a little lighter built. One Chinaman alone pulls the machine, and a very creditable pace he goes, often with two people seated inside. All the rickshaws are licensed like hackney carriages, and are very clean and well kept. The backs are often decorated with various designs in lacquer-work, depicting terrific animals in impossible positions, generally engaged in fierce combats with other equally imaginary and impossible quadrupeds. Being short of clothes, I commissioned my friend Yon Tong Lee, the tailor, to make me a suit of blue serge. He did so very satisfactorily for the sum of six dollars in the course of the day : cheap, good, and expeditious work. Most people who know anything about him seem to heartily hate the Chinaman and all his works. At first sight he appears to have many valuable qualities, but evidently most of these disappear on closer acquaintance. From Penang to Singapore we had 220 of them as deck passengers, and four or five as saloon passengers. From Singapore to Hong Kong a fresh batch of 507 came on board, three or four being first-class passengers. Having not much else to do on board, we spent the best part of a fortnight in quietly watching the Chinaman and his ways, in so far as it is possible to do so on board ship. Naturally, the first attribute one attaches to him, next to a pigtail, is opium. Our ship being an opium ship, full to the hatches with opium, and having these large numbers of Chinamen on board, it was only natural to expect that we should see the opium demon at his best, or rather worst. A little independent testimony, one way or the other, helps to elucidate any question; and here is ours. Out of the first batch of 220, all well-to-do men who had 'made their pile' and were going home, and therefore well able to afford the luxury, we could only discover two opium-smokers. Out of the second batch of 507 we could only see four. That is to say, that out of 727 Chinamen only six were opium-smokers. I must say this highly satisfactory state of affairs came to me as a revelation; for it was my privilege in England to hear a perfectly blood-curdling discourse on the subject. This discourse was on the following lines:—' My *dear* brethren, we have a monstrous and inhuman Government which forces the poor Chinaman to buy Indian opium, whereby the Indian Exchequer profits enormously. The price of Blood, my brethren! the price of Blood! Opium is at the root of all evil, and therefore we, an enlightened and Christian nation, force 300,000,000 Chinamen to become besotted and degraded individuals. Now, the least you can do, being Englishmen, and therefore in a degree responsible for this appalling wickedness, is to *subscribe freely to the China Mission* as an act of atonement;' and so on, and so on. Probably there is no country in the world more open to cheap agitations on any subject than England. But the interesting feature in the majority of these agitations is that they are directed against luxuries and comforts, and sometimes necessaries, of other people. Amongst really earnest and well-meaning Englishmen, probably no more inconsequent sect exists than that which is generally known by the name of 'the Exeter Hall party.' To us, the large body of outsiders, it is no exaggeration to say that bigotry, ignorance, and the hand of the Reverend Stiggins, rather than charity, forbearance, and common sense, appear to direct their councils. This week's mail adds another delicate item. Two English ladies, having spent a winter in India, engaged in a highly indelicate quest, arrive home with appalling stories of what they are pleased to call 'State legislation for the propagation of vice.' To combat and eradicate certain forms of disease, the wisest and most learned physicians have recommended certain preventive measures. Exeter Hall the great and good disapproves of these. In its own unctuous words, 'Divine Providence inflicts certain diseases on human nature as a punishment for certain sins,' and therefore no steps are to be taken to avert the evil. To follow this argument to its logical conclusion: cholera, smallpox, and yellow fever are punishments inflicted by the Almighty, and therefore it is excessively impious to take steps to avert them.

To eat green peas with a two-pronged fork is 'a work of supererogation and devilish long,' as the Bengali Babu puts it; but the Chinaman eats a hard-boiled egg with a pair of chopsticks. A chopstick is rather thinner than a cedar pencil, and about twice as long. He eats everything—rice, fish, meat, vegetables—out of a dozen little dishes, but all with the inevitable chopstick. He does not drink his tea or beer, however, with a chopstick. In his tea he will put anything handy—rice, sliced carrot, or bread. Bottled beer he drinks frequently, but in small quantities, and out of a small bowl. Both in smoking tobacco and smoking opium he is a most uncomfortable individual. When you or I sit down to smoke, we like a fairly long, peaceful spell of it, and a pipe or cigar that draws well is a *sine quâ non*. Not so our friend the heathen. In smoking tobacco he has so small a bowl to his pipe that he can only take two whiffs and it is finished: then a long string of elaborate preparations to refill and light it. Two more whiffs and out it goes again; and so on *ad infinitum*. With opium the process of preparation is much longer and the brief puff just as short; moreover, the pipe *never* seems to draw properly. Just as the gentleman—according to fancy portraits of him—with a beatific smile on his countenance, should be gently lulled to sleep in the arms of imaginary houris, or whatever a Chinaman calls them, he is in reality engaged in digging a long pin into his pipe to make it draw properly. Times out of number we have watched them, and not once did a gentleman get through his two whiffs without having recourse to the long pin.

A hundred and eighty miles south of Hong Kong the engines broke down; but luckily, though we were in the direct track of typhoons, it was perfectly calm for the ten hours we lay helpless. During the whole voyage from Calcutta, with the exception of the first two days, the sea and weather were all that could be desired.

On June 12th, passing through a thirty-mile labyrinth of islands, we turned a sharp corner, and found ourselves face to face with the beautiful town of Hong Kong. Here we had to leave the good ship *Catherine Apcar* and our kind friend Captain Olifent. It is impossible to help comparing the kindness and attention one receives on these non-professional passenger ships with the want of either often experienced on the large regular liners. I have now arrived at that mature age when to be treated with rather less consideration than an ordinary Gladstone bag is a distinct grievance to me. To pay £4 *per diem* for the honour and privilege of being herded like cattle in a pen, in a fashionable ship, is not my idea of happiness at sea. By the way, I calculate that the chief steward on a big steamer is worth £1200 a year in tips. Here is a fine and hitherto unexplored opening for the numerous younger sons of *paterfamilias*.

CHAPTER IV

THE NAPLES OF THE EAST

THE steam-launch from the Hong Kong Hotel meets all ships, and no sea-worn traveller can do better than step straight on board of it. The hotel is one of the best I have come across in Asia, and recalls to memory the large and well-managed hotels of Europe. The rooms are excellent: large, well furnished, and well appointed. Ours was on the fourth story, at a corner, where we caught every cooling breeze, and from the veranda of which we could command a splendid view of the harbour and mainland. The charges seem high, till one realises the fact that a dollar is not 4s. 4d. now, but only 2s. 6d. All charges are made in dollars. For our room, with board and all extras, the charge was five dollars a head a day.

In Singapore it is considered the height

of wickedness to ride in a rickshaw, and no resident would dream of appearing in one. At Hong Kong, however, horsed conveyances are not obtainable on the spur of the moment, and therefore the choice remains between riding in a rickshaw or being carried in a 'chair.' Any one with the least proper pride, however, will not be seen in a rickshaw, or certainly not a public rickshaw. To be thoroughly *chic*, a 'chair,' the ancient 'jampan' of India, is quite necessary. We saw very few ladies in rickshaws; all were being carried about in solemn pomp, at the rate of two miles an hour, in chairs. Perhaps a rickshaw is looked upon as a fast and un-ladylike conveyance; perchance it is regarded much as our grandmothers regarded a hansom cab. In India the tide is the other way.

In the evening we drove down to the race-course—a very nice one too: but where on earth the ponies, or horses, come from to race, it is impossible to conjecture. During our stay in Hong Kong we saw, first and last, perhaps a dozen ponies; and a man of ordinary activity could have run faster than any one of these could gallop. The China pony is not unlike the Kabuli pony, but with straight, heavy shoulder, and absolutely impossible paces. A resident told me that he had had four in as many years, and none of them could stand on their legs at all, at any pace faster than a walk. Polo, of a sort, is played; but the ponies, as I said before, are impossible. A beautiful graveyard, admirably kept, faces the race-course. Most of the graves are those of soldiers and sailors—memorials of epidemics and shipwrecks. We noticed one column erected to the memory of 21 sergeants, 1 drummer, 18 women, 106 children, and 466 men of the 59th Regiment, who died in China. Another simply stated that it was 'sacred to the memory of Mary,' with no other inscription, or date.

The Sikh police are in full evidence in the streets, and, after dark, mount with carbines and ball ammunition. A policeman's life does not seem to suit our old friend the Singh. He is so large and lethargic by nature, that the professional dawdle of a policeman gives him a sloppy look. The damp heat, too, is against him, and he has the appearance of one whose back is about to break. As far as his duties go, he is, I believe, an eminent success.

Driving back to the hotel, the following signboard appeared conspicuously in one street :—

> **LONG WA**
> SCULPTOR AND STONE MASON
> 179 MONUMENTS *ALWAYS*
> ON HAND

Apropos of signboards and things sepulchral, here are two which face each other in a small street near the railway station in Portsmouth :—

> **J. SMITH**
> THE MAN THAT DYES
> THAT HE MAY
> LIVE

> **T. JONES**
> THE MAN THAT LIVES
> THAT HE MAY
> DYE

It demonstrated gross ignorance, but we were surprised to find that the official name for Hong Kong is Victoria; perhaps other people who have not visited it are unaware of the fact. Victoria or Hong Kong is an island, and the town lies at the foot of a steep green hill on the borders of a perfectly land-locked lagoon, one of the finest harbours in the world. All the shops and the whole of the business portion of the colony are in the town, at the water's level; but the houses of those who can afford it are on the Peak, the name of the afore-mentioned hill. On this ridge are two very fine hotels; and the settlement on 'topside,' as the Chinaman calls it, is connected with the town below by a cable tramway. This tramway runs perfectly straight up an almost perpendicular hill, working on the principle of an endless cable; the down car, as it descends, pulls up the other car. If the cable breaks—and the possibility prominently forces itself on the traveller's attention as his toes gradually rise to a level with the top of his head—both cars, it might be expected, would, with more or less velocity, boom like an avalanche through the town, and make straight to the sea. As a matter of fact, they say that the brakes are so strong that the car can be stopped dead at the steepest part, even with a broken cable. Unenterprising strangers would, no doubt, rather watch the experiment from the top of the hill. The ascent takes ten minutes, and trams run every quarter of an hour. On the Peak, which is about 2000 ft. above sea-level, the climate is delightful—certainly 10° cooler than it is in the town below; and the prospect in every direction is enchanting. There are many worse places in this wicked world than Hong Kong.

The garrison consists of one British infantry regiment, one or two batteries, some sappers, and the Hong Kong Regiment. Here, as at Singapore, great groaning is going on over what is called the 'military contribution,' that is, the sum exacted from the colony for the support of the garrison. 'We don't want any of your soldiers here—the fleet is enough for us,' said a leading merchant to me. Of course, he knew best. Later, at dinner, I happened to ask why all the troops were garrisoned in the close, hot town, instead of on the airy and salubrious Peak. 'Bless you, there are 200,000 Chinamen in this town to be kept in order!' said the same member. Whereat there was a general laugh all round. As at Singapore, a commander-in-chief sways the sceptre over this diminutive force; and a governor sways another sceptre over him. Looking out from our commanding position at the hotel, it was a somewhat striking fact that the only British men-of-war in harbour were an obsolete old wooden three-decker, built in the year A.D. 1, and called the *Victor Emmanuel*; and a diminutive gunboat, about the size of a junk. Close alongside H.M.S. *Victor Emmanuel* lay a fair-sized modern French man-of-war, which could have sunk her in three minutes; whilst three other good-sized war-vessels of the same nationality lay close by. If war had been declared whilst we were looking out of the window, it would have been a poor

The Naples of the East

look-out for Hong Kong at the commencement of hostilities. Both entrances to the harbour are, however, no doubt thoroughly prepared with submarine mines, torpedoes, and the remaining delights of naval warfare; so that the Frenchman's triumph would be short. At the same time, I felt much in prospective for the proprietors of the Hong Kong Hotel: it is so very prominent, and just a nice range from the anchorage of the foreign men-of-war.

At the hotel all the servants, including the chambermaids, are Chinamen; and very good servants they seem to make. The hopeless squalor of an Indian hotel is entirely absent, and the Chinaman keeps everything as clean as an English servant. One Chinaman does as much work as three Indian servants, and draws from two to three times as much pay. The waiters wear long white nightgowns, and look like ghosts with pigtails.

There are some very good European shops in the town, and of course crowds of Chinese tradesmen. Evidently a chemist's shop pays well, for there are five within shouting distance of the hotel. We found nothing much to tempt us except a few small silver ornaments, a Chinese *chou* dog —quite black, tongue and all—and basket-chairs, which are made in every variety of form and shape. Many of the designs are beautiful, and the work is excellent. They cost from one to four dollars each. The *chou* dog cost a dollar and a half, and went back to India with us. A curious custom with regard to the coinage is met with. Such a large number of counterfeit dollars are in circulation that the bank punches its own brand on all the good dollars: this punching process, besides stamping some Chinese words on the silver, from the force of the blow makes the dollar into a little bowl. These 'chopped' dollars, as they are called, with a handle fixed to them make unique spoons. In Shanghai they will not look at chopped dollars: a paper dollar, or a 'clean' Mexican, is considered the safest.

Hong Kong is only three days' sail from Manilla; therefore, 1 re are to be found

PLEASE OBSERVE THE NAILS

Manilla cigars at their best and cheapest. They vary from one and a half dollars to six dollars a hundred. An excellent cigar can be had at the rate of three dollars a hundred. It seems impossible to get a good Manilla cigar in England, or in India; yet here they are, of the finest quality, and simply pining for purchasers. I have heard it gravely stated that there is opium in Manilla cigars, and that consequently they give you a headache. As my friend the tobacconist remarked, 'they would be worth a shilling a-piece if there was opium in them : opium is as dear as gold.'

We were much tempted to continue our journey to Yokohama by the *Empress of China*, one of the magnificent new ships running in connection with the Canadian Pacific Railway; but unfortunately the return journey would not fit in, so we decided for the Messageries Maritimes line. We chanced across the *Caledonien*, a very large and comfortable ship with only six first-class passengers on board. To give some idea of the roominess on board, it may be mentioned that the promenade-deck is 108 yards long! Of course, we had our choice of fifty cabins; and two stewardesses and about a dozen stewards hovered around to minister to our wants. There is nothing like an empty ship for comfort. The *cuisine* on board was excellent; and light wines, beers, whiskies-and-soda, and other similar drinks are free. Usually at sea it appears to be necessary—heaven only knows why!—to have meals at all and the most unusual and uncomfortable hours. Breakfast at 8 A.M., lunch at 12.30 P.M., tea at 3 P.M., and dinner at 6 P.M. On the *Caledonien* all feasts except dinner were movable; for instance, breakfast was to be obtained from 9 to 11 A.M., and lunch from 1 to 2.30 P.M. This added much to one's comfort. We came across a curious instance of the cosmopolitan nature of the English language. We were the only English people on board, the others being French, Dutch, Danish, Russian, and Japanese; and yet we heard all these foreigners constantly talking English amongst themselves—not in the least out of compliment to us, but for their own convenience. I could not find any one to talk French to except the Chinese pantry-man: we were kindred spirits, and about equally good at the language.

We left Hong Kong on the 15th June, after a very pleasant little sojourn. My comrade, the Chinaman, on certain occasions threw overboard square bits of wood covered with writing. I asked what these were. He said they were prayers to the gods of the waters for fine weather and a smooth sea. He proved to be a most successful mediator, for the weather was beautiful, and the ship as steady as a platform.

On June 17th, towards evening, we entered the Yellow Sea, and shortly after anchored near the mouth of the Shanghai River, opposite Woosung. Here is a Chinese fort, which commands the entrance. It is armed with modern guns, and may possibly be more formidable than it looks. The sea is called Yellow from its supposed colour. Some of the passengers immediately discovered that it really was bright yellow : as a matter of fact, the colour is much that of our ancient friend the Thames—mud, pure mud colour. A steam-launch took us and the mails up the river to Shanghai, a run of one and a half hours. We passed a great many war-ships, English and Chinese predominating. Of the latter we counted ten—five good-sized ships with formidable-looking rams, and five gunboats. Our Chinese guide later informed us, 'Chinamen. 300 ships got it;' the other 290 were apparently away for a holiday. We put up at the Hôtel des Colonies, not a very commodious or comfortable hotel, and very noisy. It was hardly possible to sleep all night from the din of passing traffic and rickshaw-men shouting. Before breakfast we went off in rickshaws, piloted by a Chinese guide, to see 'China town,' the Chinese city of Shanghai. After the first hundred yards we had to leave our conveyances and walk, the streets being about two yards wide and roughly paved. As far as sanitation or structural improvement goes, probably Shanghai has stood still for two thousand years. Crooked little streets with tawdry or squalid-looking shops, tea-houses dirty and uninviting; and over all broods a subtle and poisonous odour which ought, according to our ideas of sanitation, to kill off the inhabitants in swarms. Our guide took us to the main joss-house, or temple, and showed us 'the first three man, now plenty full men.' They were made of burnished brass, and were supposed to be the first three people created, since which, as the guide truly remarked, the world has got 'plenty full' of men. He also took us to a curious old tea-garden right in the heart of the city, where miniature rockeries of quaint forms were festooned about amidst a few bushes. At one corner stood the tea-house. We asked who it belonged to, and our guide answered, 'First belong big mandarin, he go bad and have his head cut off, now belong Shanghai Bank.' Let us hope the tenure of the Shanghai Bank will not have an equally tragic ending.

After breakfast we drove round the European quarter, and out to the race-course. Very flat everywhere, and not to be compared for a moment with Hong Kong in point of natural attractions. The climate, however, is, to Northern notions, during the greater part of the year excellent. In the winter there is sometimes as much as six inches of snow on the ground. In June we saw large numbers of Europeans wearing no more tropical head-covering than what the schoolboy calls a 'bowler' hat, or else the ordinary straw hat, in the middle of the day. Our guide gave us a brief and graphic account of a somewhat serious disturbance which occurred a few years ago. 'Plenty Chinaman make dead two—three Englishman,—shoot with gun. Plenty Frenchman afraid, Frenchman say " How can?" all Frenchman go on ships. English stop in house and keep flag on house. Frenchman take French flag down, and put Russian flag on house. After few days, all right.'

Amongst new sights we noticed a peculiar one-wheeled conveyance. It is like an Irish car on one wheel : two passengers sit on each side balancing each other, and one man pushes the vehicle along, like a wheelbarrow.

At midday the launch started back for the

ship, and we were much impressed by the fact that the large concourse of foreigners, men, women, and children, all insisted on talking English to each other—and very bad English too, in most cases—at the most crucial and trying moment. As the launch put off, a wild chorus of the English 'Goodbye' went up from the wharf, and was responded to from on board in the same language; yet I doubt if there was a single Englishman amongst them. One sometimes wishes that the more rabid Radicals—those whose aim and object in life would appear to be to dismember the great empire which has been raised by the genius of their forefathers—could go about the world and live about the world for a year or two. They would without a shadow of doubt return to England confirmed Conservatives on all imperial questions. It is not till we leave Europe behind, and get out into the wider world, that we begin to appreciate the immense factor that the British nation is in the prosperity of the world.

Several new passengers came on board,

amongst them a few Japanese and some American missionaries. One little Japanese lady captivated the whole ship straight away, and all the ship's officers might be discovered, in rotation, in impassioned postures before the little damsel. Even the captain unbent so far as to enter into a magnificent flirtation with her, and made trembling sailors carry her deck-chair about. Those less bold struck captivating attitudes in the offing, and hoped for favourable notice later. It is only forty hours' steam from Shanghai to the entrance of the Inland Sea of Japan; but, unfortunately, as we neared land we were enveloped in a thick fog, and for thirty-six hours drifted about without the least notion where we were. The whistle was kept constantly going, which made sleep at night difficult; and the water was too deep to anchor. We passengers, the sea being smooth, were not inconvenienced, beyond being kept so much extra time at sea; but the ship's officers had an exceedingly bad time of it, for the currents are very strong in these parts, and no sun having been seen for two days, our whereabouts was marked on the daily chart with nothing more definite than a big query. Add to this the large size and deep draught of the ship, and we can understand their anxiety.

During this temporary halt, it seemed not altogether out of place to enter into a short dissertation on the subject of towels, napkins, soap, and other media for personal purification as seen on a French ship. Soap is of course absent, conspicuously absent—that is an old international grievance; but towels and napkins are thrust under one's notice with conscious pride. No fault is to be found with either, except in regard to their relative size. The first morning on board, after soaking luxuriously for some time in a large marble bath, the panic-stricken thought occurs, 'Angels and ministers! where is the towel?' There is no bell, and to yell out of the door is to match one's voice against the ship's engines. A passing sailor happily supplies the missing link: 'Une serviette, s'il vous plait;—er—hem—er—disez au garçon.' He is an intelligent youth, and understands. The *garçon* arrives, smiling politely. 'Mais le voilà la serviette, monsieur!' and from under a pile of pyjamas and dressing-gowns he produces a neatly folded little article, exactly two and a half feet square, and very thin. This is the bath-towel. Absurdly enough, we had mistaken it for a stray duster. At breakfast, on the other hand, we are treated with alarming liberality. Ladies are let off more easily, but the more powerful sex is expected to grapple with a napkin which would make a creditable flying-jib for a five-ton yacht. Having once unfolded one of these luxurious—and prodigal—insignia, it requires at least two men of active habits to fold it again. A facetious fellow, probably hailing from that perfidious Albion, once accounted for this curious phenomenon by declaring that our Gallic neighbour executed his most elaborated ablutions in his finger-bowl ; whilst the large marble bath was merely a fashionable toy, into which to thrust a foot or two in daily dalliance. Hence the proportion of drying materials allowed at each of the two functions. Such an explanation would, of course, be a libel nowadays :

perhaps, though, the matter is a relic of a time when such things were possible.

These interesting remarks were suddenly interrupted by the fog lifting and showing that we were close to, and running straight on to, a perfectly precipitous wall of rock—this was our introduction to JAPAN. Happily, the water is deep right up to the land, so we had time to scoop round—or whatever sailors call it—and stand out to sea. On investigating the charts, it was found that we had hit off the coast some sixty miles out of our course. Everything was plain sailing now, and by midnight we were in the far-famed Inland Sea.

Here is another addition to my collection of notices: it faced us all day as we sat on the poop admiring the scenery, and forms an elegant contrast between the superabundant politeness of the French language and the severe directness of the Anglo-Saxon dialect:

> Les Parents sont priés de ne pas laisser monter les Enfants ICI.
>
> Children not allowed here.

CHAPTER V

JAPAN—ON FIRST ACQUAINTANCE

THE captain said that he had passed through the Inland Sea forty-five times, and only twice had he experienced fine weather. We were therefore fully prepared for anything but fine weather, and were not altogether disappointed. The sea is 240 miles long, its greatest width being 40 miles, but throughout its length it is constantly broken up by groups of small islands. All round these is deep water, so that ships of the largest tonnage steam at full speed in and out, and pass quite close to them. Perhaps writers and narrators have exaggerated the narrowness and intricacy of these passages; or perhaps one's own imagination had exaggerated them in anticipation. The vision in one's mind was of a huge ship just squeezing through between two islands, the captain calmly plucking a leaf from one, whilst the mate judiciously expectorated on a roof on the opposite shore. Indeed, three minutes before we made the passage of the narrowest part, an old traveller staked his reputation on the assertion that it was not more than 100 yards wide. This was rather a come-down, but even 100 yards was rather narrow for a big ship. A sea-captain also told us that the ship ran full speed at a lofty and beetling cliff; and just as you were about to say your prayers and settle into your lifebelt, the ship slewed round on her own axis, and went through a passage so narrow, one could hardly see it. That also was quite good enough for us. The reality, though certainly picturesque and interesting, did not come up to these high ideals. The narrowest channel passed through was at least 500 yards wide, with green sloping islands on either side. Probably the entrance to Singapore harbour, from the Penang direction, is only a few yards broader, and equally picturesque. All the morning, though dull and rather cold, we sat in much luxury, wrapped up in great-coats and rugs, and watched the new and interesting panorama which passed before us. The sea is nothing but a huge lake, as smooth as ice and curiously reflective. Hundreds of fishing-boats dotted the waters, full of little idle men, all seeming to have nothing to do but sit about and laugh. Great two-masted sailing junks lay lazily on the still sea, as if the reaching of any destination was a matter of the very smallest importance. The villages—brought quite close by field-glasses—clean and neat, with their wooden houses black-roofed, and with the great cedar-tree in the middle, seemed absolutely deserted; or perhaps all the merry little inhabitants were taking their cheerful little siestas. Everywhere was an intense stillness and peace, and only a bright sun was required to make the picture perfect. We see such pictures on the Italian lakes and the little seas of Switzerland. One might almost be there: a little change in the shape of the sails, a little more colouring in costume, a little more whitewash on the cottages, and the transformation would be complete.

The western end of the sea is more varied and picturesque than the eastern, though perhaps the incessant rain rather damped one's appreciation as the ship sped on her way eastwards. Towards evening we rounded Hiogo Point, and entered the harbour of Kobé; our ship running up alongside a jetty with her bows within fifty yards of the beach, so deep is the water within a few yards of the shore. The towns of Hiogo and Kobé adjoin one another, and strew the shores of two small bays. Behind the town rise abruptly green, pleasant-looking, fir-crowned hills; their lower slopes dotted with European-built houses. A good hotel, the Oriental, is within a few minutes' walk of the wharf.

After dinner we landed, and made our first acquaintance with the man of Japan in his own country. The particular man we first met was a rickshaw-man; but he might have been nothing lower than a Lord Chamberlain from the depth and grace of the bows with which he greeted us. It seemed more fitting that he should sit inside the rickshaw and allow himself to be drawn; but he would not hear of this. With much bowing and salutation and superb flourishes of the hat, we finally seated ourselves, and were whisked off at a rapid rate down the street. At night, and by the light of the lamps, everything and everybody looked just as if they had walked out of the painted screens and fans and scrolls we are all so familiar with. The 'pot' hats and deer-stalker caps, which in the daytime disfigure so many of the men, were not visible at night. All we could see were dainty little people, all dressed in the national costume, all with large paper umbrellas, and all toddling along on high clogs—for the rain was still falling gently. As we looked into the shops, cosy little parties sat round the braziers in mid-floor, and laughed and talked and smoked little pipes and played on little guitars. After an hour or so we went on board again, and my tender of 20 cents for his trouble to the Lord Chamberlain was received with renewed and still more profound bows. For 40 cents, at this rate, a guard of honour and a band would assuredly be supplied. Talking of guards of honour reminds me of the one we saw at Hong Kong. It was composed of Chinese military police, drawn up, as is not unusual with guards of honour, in two lines facing each other. When the bigwig arrived, instead of the order 'Present arms,' or whatever the Chinese equivalent is, being given, the gentleman in command evidently said, 'By your right—Prepare to bow!— — —Bow!' Whereupon the whole guard of honour set to work bowing and scraping, a sort of *feu de joie* of salutations—down one line, up the next, backwards and forwards—a perfect hurricane of politeness. The word politeness leads me into another Chinese recollection. The Japanese are the pink of politeness as far as outward forms go, but the Chinaman, if he really wishes to be civil to you, goes deeper: he panders solidly to your vanity—the highest form of politeness. He says, 'How is your excellency, and how are those charming little cherry-cheeked cherubs of your lordship, the beautiful little angels?' 'Quite well, thank you; and how are that nice little boy and girl of yours?' 'Augh! pough! wretched little ugly demons, *they* are not worth mentioning!' Observe the subtle flattery! Everything and anything that belongs to you, down to that pudding-faced freckly boy, is angelic. Everything and anything that belongs to himself is, for conversational purposes, debased to the lowest possible comparative stratum.

However, this has nothing on earth to do with Japan. Let us get back to Kobé. Motomachi is the name of the principal street in the Japanese town, in which are to be found all the best shops for buying curios and odds-and-ends. Not one of the least of the merits of these dealers is that they do not in the least resent your buying nothing. They show all they have with pleasure, and merely add to their parting salutation, 'Please come again.' For those who are making any lengthened stay in Japan it is of course better to wait till experience has taught them what are the best things to buy, and what are the proper prices to pay for them. But those who are in a hurry cannot do better than go to Hamada's Fine Art Depôt, where all the prices are fixed, and the foreigner may be sure of getting his money's worth.

Dividing Hiogo from Kobé is an extraordinary river, the Minato-gawa. It runs to the sea along a raised causeway, twenty or thirty feet above the level of the two towns. It looks like a canal, with high embankments, crossing a shallow valley. Apparently what has happened is this. The river in ordinary times is a mere stream, but in flood-time it becomes a roaring torrent. To save themselves from its vagaries, the inhabitants elevated the banks. The silt from above soon filled up this channel, and the bank had again to be raised. And so on till the river reached its present exalted position. This has all happened since A.D. 1100, when the original course of the river was artificially altered. The journey from Kobé to Yokohama occupies twenty hours by rail, or twenty-five to thirty hours by sea. We went round by sea, and were well repaid by a beautiful day, and very enchanting views of the coast-line, with the magnificent and solitary Mount Fuji in the background. This mountain, familiar to all in Japanese pictures, has a peculiar grandeur, enhanced by its small surroundings. As some writer says, 'it rises with one majestic sweep' from the plain. Any child could draw a picture of it: an obtuse-angled triangle with the top angle cut off, and sugared with snow. The highest point is about 12,450 feet above sea-level.

Yokohama might be any small seaport in the United Kingdom, with a few rickshaws thrown in. In the back streets Japanese vendors have accumulated round the nucleus of European civilisation, but the place is essentially not Japanese. Unless, therefore, the visitor has come to Japan to buy curios at vast prices at European shops, a few hours only of Yokohama will suffice. There is one valuable purchase, however, to be made which will add vastly to the tourist's comfort and instruction, and that is *Murray's Handbook*. It is compiled from the contributions of several distinguished authorities thoroughly cognisant of the land and its people. A little experience in Eastern travel, and Murray's book, make the services of the 'pestilential guide' unnecessary in Japan. It is impossible to carry about many books when travelling lightly; but Mitford's charming little *Tales of Old Japan*, and *Things Japanese* by Professor Chamberlain, would squeeze in anywhere. To read Mitford's tale of the *Forty-seven Ronins*, and then to visit the scene of their death, is one of those intellectual feasts which go to make up the charm of travel. Professor Chamberlain's book is a fund of quiet humour, combined with solid instruction, from beginning to end.

This was the end of June, and the weather had cleared and become bright and fine. The heat was nothing more than that of a hot summer's day in England, 73° to 75°; but we heard the inhabitants groaning, and saw punkahs at dinner-time in some private houses.

Before proceeding into the interior, passports have to be obtained through the consul. The documents generally take three or four days to make out, but meanwhile the traveller is at liberty to move about within twenty-four miles of Yokohama. In this radius is included Tokyo, formerly called Yedo, the capital, and a thoroughly Japanese city. It covers an area estimated at half as large as that of London, with a population of 1,300,000.

CHAPTER VI

JAPANESE CITY LIFE

'WHEN Greek meets Greek, then comes the tug of war.' When Mr. Clement Scott and Sir Edwin Arnold agree to differ on such an important matter as the women of Japan, heaven help the women! The first sentence, in the first leading article, in the first newspaper which met our view in Japan alluded to this interesting difference of opinion in no uncertain language. Sir Edwin Arnold, as we all know, considers the Japanese women as only a little lower than the angels, and of course infinitely superior to Western types of beauty and grace. Mr. Scott, from his recent poem in one of the Chinese papers, appears to have travelled from the other end of the world with the express purpose of differing in as pronounced a manner as possible from Sir Edwin. The Japanese, like all young nations

—for young they are as a civilised people—are peculiarly sensitive to outside criticism. If Sir Edwin Arnold considered them perfect, he was, to Japanese notions, quite welcome to his opinions; and he very naturally made many friends, not only for himself but for his countrymen, by giving expression to his views. Mr. Clement Scott had, judging from his poem, nothing too bad and nothing too personally uncomplimentary to say of Japanese ladies. He also was perfectly within his right to have his own opinions; but the expression of them has made him and his countrymen temporarily somewhat unpopular. It will occur to ordinary people that a newspaper ode on such a subject can hardly hope to lead to any amendment; the Japanese woman will not become more beautiful, nor taller, nor slimmer, because she is told with candid directness that she is fat, podgy, and ugly. The general feeling in English circles in China and Japan is evidently against Mr. Clement Scott, though hardly prepared to subscribe to the enthusiasm of Sir Edwin Arnold.

Perhaps the views of old European residents are best summed up in Mr. Mitford's[1] judicious words: 'Not beautiful, these damsels, if judged by our standard; but the charm of Japanese women lies in their manner and their dainty little ways.' Probably most travellers, too, will agree with Mr. Mitford. It seems that to compare Japanese women with European women is to compare things which are not open to comparison. As well might we attempt to compare the stag with the gazelle, or an 80-ton gun with a battery of Horse Artillery.

One of the best places to study the town life of the people is Tokyo, anciently Yedo or Yeddo. The capital of the empire, and the residence of the sovereign, here is to be seen that modern Japan which has sprung up with such surprising rapidity within the last twenty years. The conception of the Mikado accepted by most Englishmen is probably strictly in accordance with that suggested by Messrs. Gilbert and Sullivan's operetta: a haughty autocrat, magnificently dressed

Tales of Old Japan, by A. B. Mitford.

like a figure on a Japanese plate, and simply bristling with long knives; his eyebrows pointing to heaven at an angle of 45°, and the corners of his mouth to—the opposite place at a corresponding angle. No sensible person would doubt that he went about in state, seated in a huge bullock-cart like a demi-god, surrounded by daimios, and ronins, and shoguns, and with refreshing impartiality invited any stray person to commit *hara-kiri*[1] on the smallest provocation. Noticing in the *Japan Mail* (published in English) that his Majesty would issue from his palace at 8.30 one morning, in order to visit the Cadets' Riding School—(fancy a Cadet, and still better a Riding School! one might be at Woolwich!)—we made our way to the main gate in order to feast our eyes on the terrible person of our imaginings. At 8.30 punctually issued an outrider in a gold-bound top-hat, mounted on a showy little half-bred chestnut Arab, and supported on either side by two mounted gentlemen in French uniform—probably *aides-de-camp*.

[1] Suicide by disembowelling.

Next came part of the escort dressed as French lancers, and mounted on small black cobs about fourteen hands high. Then the *pièce de résistance*, the Mikado himself: but—imagine our grief and dismay! —also in a French uniform, and seated in an ordinary closed landau. The rest of the escort followed, and then came two or three carriages containing gentlemen in frock-coats or European uniforms: possibly the terrible daimios[1] of twenty years ago, with their wings clipped, and disguised as marquises and counts. I, for one, am all for progress and enlightenment; but wearing other people's clothes is neither enlightened nor progressive. To meet a daimio in a frock-coat was as great a shock to me as it would be to meet my revered parent in Oxford Street attired as a Chippeway Indian. Let us have progress, by all means; but for heaven's sake let us stick to our own clothes.

Now that I am on clothes, the Muse may as well work herself out. The streets of Tokyo are to the foreigner simply ruined by

[1] Great and powerful feudal lords

the hats. Nine-tenths of the men of the middle classes, though wearing the national costume as far as their body garments and feet are concerned, insist on surmounting the structure with a European hat—'a bowler,' soft felt, or straw being the favourite shapes. The women met with in the streets are, almost without an exception, dressed as we see them pictured, and we begin to feel that we have not travelled in vain; but some of the great ladies of the palace, I believe, dress in European frocks and bonnets. We saw a party of them at the theatre: I felt inclined to beg and beseech them to go home and come back dressed like all the charming little figures around them. A Japanese lady in a Paris bonnet and London dress brings herself within the clutches of Mr. Clement Scott's most severe criticism. In the same way, most European ladies in Japanese costumes are apt to look like very stout individuals in very skimpy dressing-gowns. Farsari, the great photographer, was telling us that many European and American ladies come to him to be photographed in Japanese dresses, and all expect to come out the graceful little toy figures one sees about in Japan. The European lady in a Japanese costume, therefore, on the other hand, would be a fit subject for a counterblast of disparagement. We saw some appalling photographic specimens of both species. Amongst the children, the little girls are dressed rigidly according to the Japanese fashion, like their ma's; but the little boys, like their pa's, are running after strange gods. Whether it is a naval school, or merely a national school, they attend, I know not; but the great number of very small boys who wear very large naval officers' caps with white tops is astonishing. The ambition of every modern Japanese male is to get into a uniform of some description—military, naval, tramway, railway, or police. In this respect we must give our friend the Celestial every credit. Probably no one has ever seen a Chinaman in a French uniform, or even a frock-coat.

One cannot fail to be struck in Tokyo

with the substantial as apart from the ephemeral signs of civilisation : the network of telegraph wires, the lines of tramways, and the busy 'bus; the good postal arrangements, with fleet-footed postmen running rapidly to every quarter; telegraph boys on bicycles; at every corner a policeman in white uniform, with peaked forage-cap bound with yellow and black, and armed with a short sword; the orderly ranks of rickshaws, at licensed standings, and the rickshaw men uniformly clad, neat, willing, and obliging; the main roads broad, clean, and very fairly kept, and even the by-streets not very narrow, and much cleaner than in most large towns, whether in Asia or Europe; the shop-people civil, obliging, and open to an offer; large buildings cropping up in every direction, and electric lights at the hotels; newspaper boys bustling about in every direction, and board schools full of children; a good club, fine museum, and palatial barracks, and large, well-managed hotels;—all these elements of civilisation speak for themselves, and emphasise the extraordinarily adaptive nature of the Japanese character. Whilst China has stood still for twenty centuries, twenty short years have been sufficient to produce all these changes in Japan. Still more wonderful, these innovations are not, as is usual with other Eastern nations, shoddy imitations of the real thing; they are genuine articles. The railways are well managed and well ordered, and the trains comfortable, clean, and punctual. The postal and telegraph services are, I am informed, as good and reliable as those of most European nations; and experts assure me that the navy is really an efficient service, and studies closely its model and guiding star, the British navy. The only qualm that occasionally crosses one's mind is, 'Where does all the money come from?' However, that is no business of ours. We can but wish prosperity to a nation young in civilisation, but which has already become an important factor in the politics of the East. I had an opportunity a few years ago of examining Siamese civilisation : that was what might be called spurious civilisation, in its thoroughly Eastern form.

Perhaps the best place to see the townfolk in Tokyo is Asakusa, in the vicinity of the temple called Sensoji. This large temple is surrounded by booths and tea-houses, and is approached by two long streets, lined, the one with little shops in which are sold cheap finery, confectionery, smoking-comforts, and odds-and-ends, and the other with shooting-galleries, waxworks, baths, and the many other cheap amusements usually to be found at a fair. Murray's description is excellent, and describes the scene exactly: 'It is the great holiday resort of the middle and lower classes, and nothing is more striking than the juxtaposition of piety and pleasure, of gorgeous altars and grotesque ex-votos, of pretty costumes and dingy idols, the clatter of clogs, cocks and hens and pigeons strutting about among the worshippers, children playing, soldiers smoking, believers chaffering with the dealers of charms, ancient art, modern advertisements—in fine, a spectacle than which surely nothing more motley was ever witnessed within a religious edifice.' Professor Chamberlain, speaking of the Japanese religion, says: 'The Japanese, as has been often remarked, take their religion lightly. Narita, Ise, and other favourite goals of piety are equally noted for the distractions which they provide of an evening. Nor is much inquiry made into the doctrines held at any special shrine. Kompira was Buddhist and is now Shinto, having been made so by order of Government during the present reign. . . . When tradesmen of any standing join a pilgrim association, they mostly do so in order to extend their business connection and to see new places cheaply and sociably.' Inside the temple, apart from the people, one of the objects which is most striking to the ordinary observer is the immense money-box, some thirty feet long by fifteen feet broad, into which the people cast their alms. This money-chest is placed straight in front of the main altar, and is so deep that the sound of men raking up the coppers below comes as from a deep cellar. The flow of votaries goes on from morning till night, from year's end to year's end, and the shower of offerings seems to go on continuously. The wealth of a temple like this must be fabulous. Close to the money-box on the right is a wooden idol, with his features and parts of his person completely worn away, and around his neck many red bibs. This is Binzuru. Now, Binzuru was a gentleman who, though he had taken the vow of chastity, so far forgot himself as to pass a remark on the beauty of one of the lady votaries. For this highly reprehensible conduct, it was ordered by Buddha that he should be placed outside the chancel; but, by way of tempering the wind to the shorn lamb, to him was ascribed the useful attribute of having the automatic power of curing all diseases. The true believer has, for instance, only to rub Binzuru's jaw, and then his own, to be immediately cured of the toothache. As we stood by we saw him in constant use: some had head-aches, some back-aches, some leg-aches, some stomach-aches, and some aches all over. One poor old woman who could hardly totter, and was evidently in pain all over, took Binzuru piecemeal, and rubbed every portion of his person, and then the corresponding portions of her own; then, throwing a coin to the attendant, she hobbled briskly away. Such is the power of faith. The only one who had no faith was a baby, who arrived smiling and happy, but, being severely dabbed in the face by the nursemaid, possibly to cure it of future ills, set to work and howled like a wilderness. The red bibs which are placed round Binzuru's neck are the offerings of devout worshippers. Close to the temple is a colossal revolving bookcase protected by a wooden shed. This bookcase contains 6771 volumes of Buddhist scriptural literature. To read such a large number of books being rightly considered impossible, it is decreed that whoever shall thrice revolve the gigantic bookcase shall be credited with having read the whole of its contents. It turns fairly easily, and a stout man can in this way get through 6771 volumes of a foreign language in about a minute and a half. I credited myself with 1128½ books, and left, feeling that I had done a fair day's work.

CHAPTER VII

CITY LIFE—THE THEATRE

WE were fortunate enough to be in Tokyo, and to get seats at the theatre for a Japanese play, or rather series of plays lasting through the day, the Irving of Japan being the chief actor. We had considerable difficulty in getting seats, and that several days beforehand, for the sum of four dollars, —the usual charge for a seat being twenty cents. It was four dollars well expended, however, for seldom had we spent a more pleasant and interesting afternoon. The dramatic day, in each case, began at 11 A.M. and lasted till 8 P.M. The theatre is square, with a long and capacious stage running along one side of it. The audience occupy the floor and the three remaining sides, as well as two tiers, corresponding to our dress circle and gallery. The whole house throughout is divided into square pens, with just room enough to hold four people in each, and every one sits on the floor. The divisions between these pens are about a foot high, and access to one's seat is gained along elevated gangways which traverse the theatre at intervals. Out of deference to our national custom, we were courteously allowed chairs, so placed as not to interfere with the view of our neighbours. Five ladies of the court, dressed in European costumes, also were seated on chairs. The stage, unlike the usual Japanese revolving stage, is a fixed one, and a huge curtain, tastefully painted with a winter scene, hangs before it, as in our theatres. The actors, instead of entering the stage from the wings, or back of the stage, make their appearance from behind the audience, walking along a broad causeway constructed on a level with the heads of the people in the stalls. The exit, except for dead men, is by the same causeway. Dead men—and there were many of them before the day was over—were either pushed over into a dismal-looking hole at the corner of the stage, or else got up and walked out, screened by a super with a black sheet. These supers, or stage attendants, were one of the most curious items in the stage management. They were dressed in coal-black garments from head to foot, and wore heavy black veils over their faces. It was some time before we discovered what they were; at first we thought they were demoniacal spirits, supposed to pervade the atmosphere of the play. Next we decided that they were stage villains cruising round on the look-out for some one to kill. It was only after the play had partly run its course that we discovered that they were merely agents for shifting furniture, assisting corpses off the stage, and general utility servants—their dress merely signifying that, in the indulgent eyes of the audience, they were not supposed to exist. For the best part of half an hour we had watched one of these sombre figures stalking a great daimio, the hero of the piece, with a three-legged stool. Every second we expected to see the hero brained; and the anti-climax which occurred when we found he was only going to place it for his lord to sit upon moved us to a few generous tears. Talking of tears, it was quite pathetic to notice how very much to heart all the tender little ladies in the audience took the misfortunes of the actors. Some of them must have spent the greater part of the day in weeping silently, but copiously.

To the left of the stage, in a position corresponding to the middle tier of stage boxes in a European theatre, but more directly facing the audience, are seated two men who are to the play what the chorus was to the Greek plays. One of them performs on a three-stringed guitar, whilst the other, in a stentorian sing-song voice, fills in all the unspoken part of the play. He reads aloud the inmost thoughts of the villain, as that interesting person sits darkly hatching treason ; he takes up the thread of the story where the actors leave it, and prepares the audience for what is to come. Somewhat in this fashion :—Enter villain ; he stalks about making stupendous strides, stops, and frowns heavily, glares at the third man from the centre of the second row in the stalls, puts his hand to his sword, half draws it, draws his feet smartly together and transfers his gaze elsewhere, thrusts back his sword and takes to his fan. Great agitation of the fan, first up, then down, then round in half sweeps, shut with a snap, opened suddenly, shut again; and then he begins to speak. But meanwhile the gist of the whole of what we should call byplay has been proclaimed aloud by the chorus, somewhat as follows: 'Here comes Karan-suke-no-suke; he strides the stage plotting deep schemes of revenge. Aha! he has hit upon it: he will at once seek out the wretched Fugetsudo and cut off his head with a single blow. But wait! that would be too noble a death for him—far too noble. Come to my aid, demons and devils, and help me to concoct some fiendish form of revenge'—and so on, and so on. In the same way the chorus fills in those joints in the story which on our stage are left to the imagination.

The three outer walls of the theatre which face the stage are composed merely of sliding screens, and these throughout the day are thrown wide open, and fresh air circulates freely through the building. Outside are refreshment-stalls of every kind and degree, from ices and delicate confectionery to bottled beer and rice and eggs. Long intervals separate the acts; and during these, nimble waiters run along the raised causeways, and deposit dinner for four here, ices for two there, and cakes and sweetmeats for all who want them. No one desecrates the scrupulous cleanliness of the neat floor matting by wearing clogs or boots inside the theatre; and for those who wish to go out and stroll about between acts the management supply sandals. We were much amused watching the boy who issued them. He took a sharp look at each person's feet as they approached along the passage, seized a pair of sandals to fit, and deftly threw them so as to fall side by side at the exact spot where the mats end and the stone-work begins.

Out of the nine hours' performance we attended for three, seeing one complete play in that time, and part of another. Considering that we could not understand a word of the language—indeed, they say few foreigners, however well versed in Japanese, can follow the words—it speaks very highly for the skill of the actors that we had not a moment of weariness during those three hours, and as the play went on obtained a very fair notion of the plot—enough, in fact, to make up a connected and fairly intelligent story. The scene opens in a poor little cottage, where two old people are weeping and wailing and evidently in great distress. Later we discover that it is for the loss of a daughter, who has suddenly disappeared, leaving her little son—a very precocious and amusing little shrimp—in their care. During the lamentations the approach of two daimios, or feudal lords, is announced, and these two magnificent beings—one old and the other young—advance majestically through the audience on to the stage. Their costumes were of the richest brocade, and so stiff with gold that they would certainly have stood upright of themselves.

Large swords—two apiece—and several handsome daggers bristled at aggressive angles from their two distinguished waists. No tinsel stage properties these, but worth solid dollars, and many thousands of them. With the two daimios came two jet-black supers or stage-helps, as before explained, each with a three-legged stool. In watching the machinations of these suspicious-looking persons we were rather in danger of losing sight of the plot of the play; but as soon as both daimios were satisfactorily perched on their stools we breathed again, and caught on to the play. Amidst general conversation the postman arrives with a parcel. Evidently this has a dangerous air about it, for no one will open it. At last the youngest and boldest of the daimios braces himself to the task, and after a good deal of back-sliding manages to undo it in the course of ten minutes or so. Within is found a woman's arm, the hand clutching tight a long scroll. General horror, during which the two poor old people recognise their lost daughter's arm. The next thing, evidently, is to get the scroll out of the dead hand, and to see what it is all about. In this endeavour the young and muscular daimio fails miserably, and none of the others will touch the gruesome limb. To the rescue the precocious little boy, who opens the hand with ease, and releases the document. General applause. Of course, we are unable to understand what is written in it; but, cognisant of the fact that suicides in Japan always leave on their persons a history of the reasons which led them to take that step, we concluded that the lady had committed suicide, and, further, that the old daimio, from his guilty expression, was at the bottom of the trouble.

At this juncture a litter arrives with a corpse on it. This proves to be the lady. Then, in response to a good deal of promiscuous praying to divers gods, the corpse is brought to life for a few minutes by applying the amputated arm to its socket. In the short respite allowed her, the corpse evidently makes it what is vulgarly called 'pretty hot' for the old daimio—who at this moment is absent—and then dies finally.

After which, being out of the show, she walks off the stage screened by the black sheet of an attendant super.

I forgot to mention that during the whole while a distinguished-looking lady, evidently the wife of the young daimio, had been sitting unobtrusively close by. At this juncture she is suddenly taken ill with violent pains, and is borne off into a room in the cottage. The young daimio immediately sticks a dagger into the wall, hangs the dead lady's scroll on it, and sets to work to pray steadily to it, regardless of the havoc he is playing with his fine clothes. His prayers are evidently answered, for, heigh! presto! the door opens—and he finds that he is the father of a fine boy. Subdued applause from the ladies of the audience. The precocious boy has, meanwhile, afforded intense amusement to his little contemporaries in the pit by neglecting his prayers at frequent intervals in order to steal to the door to see what it is all about. This domestic occurrence, highly interesting though no doubt it was, appeared to have no bearing on the play, the plot of which now began to thicken.

Return of old daimio, and an immense amount of conversation, during which the old gentleman is evidently confronted with his crimes, and explains at much length and with much dramatic play the reasons for his course of action. Needless to say, there is only one alternative open to him, and that is to commit *hara-kiri*. I believe that only one Englishman, Mr. Mitford, has ever actually been present at a genuine officially conducted case of *hara-kiri*, and that was in 1868. Readers of Japanese literature will be familiar with the fact that when a man, belonging to the noble or soldier classes, commits that which brings him within the executioner's power, he is allowed, as an act of privilege, to commit suicide instead of suffering death at the hands of the public executioner. The ceremony is carried out with the utmost punctilio, exact rules being laid down for the conduct of all concerned. The minutest details regarding the matting on the floor and the draperies on the wall are given, and every means is taken to make the act as dignified and impressive as possible. Before describing the *hara-kiri* in the play, we cannot do better than quote Mr. Mitford's unique experience :—

'The condemned man was Taki Zenzaburô, an officer of the Prince of Bizen, who gave the order to fire upon the foreign settlement at Hiogo in the month of February 1868. The ceremony, which was ordered by the Mikado himself, took place at 10.30 at night, in the temple of Seifukuji, the headquarters of the Satsuma troops at Hiogo. A witness was sent from each of the foreign legations. We were seven foreigners in all. . . . We were invited to follow the Japanese witnesses into the *hondo*, or main hall of the temple, where the ceremony was to be performed. It was an imposing scene. A large hall with a high roof, supported by dark pillars of wood. From the ceiling hung a profusion of those huge gilt lamps and ornaments peculiar to Buddhist temples. In front of the high altar, where the floor, covered with beautiful white mats, is raised some three or four inches from the ground, was laid a rug of scarlet felt. Tall candles, placed at regular intervals, gave out a dim, mysterious light, just sufficient to let all the proceedings be seen. The seven Japanese took their places on the left of the raised floor, the seven foreigners on the right. No other person was present.

'After an interval of a few minutes of anxious suspense, Taki Zenzaburô, a stalwart man, thirty-two years of age, with a noble air, walked into the hall attired in his dress of ceremony, with the peculiar hempen-cloth wings which are worn on great occasions. He was accompanied by a *kaishaku* and three officers, who wore the *jimbaori* or war surcoat with gold facings. The word *kaishaku*, it should be observed, is one to which our word *executioner* is no equivalent. The office is that of a gentleman; in many cases it is performed by a kinsman or friend of the condemned, and the relation between them is rather that of principal and second than that of victim and executioner. In this instance the *kaishaku* was a pupil of Taki Zenzaburô, and was selected by the friends of the latter from among their own number for his skill in swordsmanship. With the *kaishaku* on his left hand, Taki Zenzaburô advanced slowly towards the Japanese witnesses, and the two bowed before them; then, drawing near to the foreigners, they saluted us in the same way, perhaps even with more deference: in each case the salutation was ceremoniously returned. Slowly and with great dignity the condemned man mounted on to the raised floor, prostrated himself before the high altar twice, and seated[1] himself on the felt carpet with his back to the high altar, the *kaishaku* crouching on his left-hand side. One of the three attendant officers then came forward, bearing a stand of the kind used in temples for offerings, on which, wrapped in paper, lay the *wakizashi*, the short sword or dirk of the Japanese, nine

---

[1] Seated himself—that is, in the Japanese fashion, his knees and toes touching the ground, and his body resting on his heels. In this position, which is one of respect, he remained until his death.

inches and a half in length, with a point and edge as sharp as a razor's. This he handed, prostrating himself, to the condemned man, who received it reverently, raising it to his head with both hands, and placed it in front of himself. . . . Bowing once more, Taki Zenzaburô allowed his upper garments to slip down to his girdle, and remained naked to the waist. Carefully, according to custom, he tucked his sleeves under his knees to prevent himself falling backwards; for a noble Japanese gentleman should die falling forwards. Deliberately, with a steady hand, he took the dirk that lay before him; he looked at it wistfully, almost affectionately; for a moment he seemed to collect his thoughts for the last time, and then, stabbing himself deeply below the waist on the left-hand side, he drew the dirk slowly across to the right side, and, turning it in the wound, gave a slight cut upwards. During this sickeningly painful operation he never moved a muscle of his face. When he drew out the dirk he leaned forward and stretched out his neck; an expression of pain for the first time crossed his face, but he uttered no sound.

'At that moment the *kaishaku*, who, still crouching by his side, had been keenly watching his every movement, sprang to his feet, poised his sword for a second in the air; there was a flash, a heavy, ugly thud, a crashing fall; with one blow the head was severed from the body. . . .

'The *kaishaku* made a low bow, wiped his sword with a piece of paper which he had ready for the purpose, and retired from the raised floor.'[1]

A more impressive and appalling ceremony it is difficult to imagine: at midnight, in the half-gloomy interior of an old temple, the hardy soldier fearlessly meeting his awful doom.

To return to our theatre. In broad daylight, with all the bright faces and tasteful dresses around, vanilla cream ices and bottled beer in full view through the side screens, and five Parisian bonnets in the middle distance, the scene lost the greater

[1] Mitford's *Tales of Old Japan*.

part of its impressiveness. Yet was the acting excellent. The old daimio's *kaishaku* was the little boy, scarce five years old. At the appointed moment the little fellow, with childish inconsequence, trotted up and presented the dagger to the old noble, who was now kneeling stripped to the waist. As laid down by rule, he stabbed himself below the waist on the left side and drew the knife across. But here the dramatic effect to us was spoilt, for, instead of doing the deed in silence, as the brave fellow above, he must needs take this highly inopportune and uncomfortable moment to make a long speech. We had noted him all along as being a very garrulous and talkative old man, but with nine and a half inches of steel in his interior he fairly surpassed himself. Most people in the audience would have given twenty cents to see him pass away quietly—we would have given a dollar gladly. At last he finished, and the little fellow the *kaishaku* raised his sword to give the death-blow. Of course, his strength was not sufficient for the deed, and the poor old fellow had to seize the point and help him to cut off his own head. After much struggling they were successful between them, and the head (a false one, of course) rolled on the stage. The old man's corpse then walked off screened by a black sheet, and the play was now practically over.

It should have been mentioned that before the play commenced, three gentlemen in the costumes of the Shogun era entered, and, as far as we could understand, explained in advance the story of the coming play.

The dresses of the daimios and their retainers were magnificent, and, passing and repassing as they do to and from the stage through the audience, it is possible to admire them closely. They are the costumes we are familiar with on the best Satsuma porcelain jars and dishes. Would that we saw them about the streets instead of suits of ditto and felt hats! To any one who has a chance of seeing a good Japanese play we can honestly say, 'Go and see it, and you will thoroughly enjoy yourself.'

CHAPTER VIII

TOKYO

ONE of the most picturesque and characteristic spots in Tokyo is the main street, called Ginza, after dark. The glare of neither gas nor electricity desecrates the scene, but thousands of paper lanterns of every design, colour, and shape light up the street and shops. Even the rickshaws carry them. The side-walks are broad, and bordered with small trees; and along the coping-stone is one continuous string of pedlars, each with his little stall brightly lit up. The whole effect is charming, and crowds of passengers throng the thoroughfare. The semi-obscurity conceals the appalling 'bowler' hat, and we only see dainty little Japanese figures bargaining here and there for their little wants, or toddling along for their evening walk. If one stands still for a moment to listen, the whole street seems to resound with the click-clack of many thousand clogs. At a little distance the sound curiously resembles the chorus of myriads of frogs in a mighty marsh. One thing which disgraces the capitals of Europe, and especially the streets of London, is absent. No courtesan shows her painted face out of the quarter of the town set aside for these unfortunates: the streets in which honest folk congregate after the labour and heat of the day is over are as safe as they are at midday.

Like all town-people, the inhabitants of Tokyo on high days and holidays flock out to various resorts on the outskirts of the city. One of these, the tombs of the Forty-Seven Ronins,[1] has a pathetic interest which perhaps appeals as much to us foreigners as to the tender hearts of the people of the country. The tragedy occurred nearly two hundred years ago, yet opposite each little headstone stands a bunch of fresh evergreen, a little trough remains always filled with water for the departed spirit, and incense burns perpetually to his memory. The story

[1] A wanderer, a knight-errant, a free-lance.

is a long one, but a few lines will explain, to students of the Japanese character, the affectionate regard with which the tombs of the forty-seven are still tended. Takumi-no-Kami, the feudal lord of these forty-seven, being insulted by another great lord, attempted to slay him. But, failing in his purpose, and being taken in the act, he was ordered by the Council to perform *hara-kiri*, which he accordingly did. To avenge their master's death, the forty-seven ronins determined to kill the great lord, his enemy. After countless stratagems and months of waiting, they at last found their opportunity. On a dark, snowy night, with the wind blowing furiously, they had their last supper together, knowing well that, whether they were successful or no, their own fate was sealed. With bold intrepidity they attacked the great man's castle, and after severe fighting slew his guard, and, seizing their enemy, beheaded him. Then, neither wishing nor attempting to escape, they retired to the tomb of their old master, and there reverently placed the head of his enemy, first washing it in a little tank, which remains to this day. Here they awaited patiently their doom, knowing well what it would be. They were, in accordance with the custom of the country, sentenced to commit *hara-kiri*; and there fell those brave men, slain by their own hands, for love of their master. Their graves line the four sides of a small enclosure adjoining the tomb of their master. Here may be seen the curious Japanese custom of leaving visiting cards on the dead; for the tomb of the leader of the band is covered with visiting cards, left by his admirers on New Year's Day. Close by, for a few coppers, can be bought little china bowls with pictures on them of the more famous personages amongst the forty-seven ronins.

It scarcely comes within the scope of a light book, which merely describes a short holiday, to enter into an extended description of the magnificent temples and mausolea of Japan. Complete and exhaustive information regarding each temple is to be found in Mr. Murray's invaluable book, from the pens of the greatest authorities on these subjects. But, apart from their artistic merit, perhaps the historic interest which centres in the tombs of the great Shoguns appeals to most foreigners, certainly to most soldiers. To appreciate these wonderful monuments of the past, it is necessary to dip a little into the ancient history of Japan.

Most of us are familiar with the two titles of Tycoon [1] and Mikado, the names given to the joint-powers who ruled Japan for nearly seven centuries. The Tycoon (or Shogun [2]) was commander-in-chief of the army, and the real ruler of the country. The Mikado was for all these centuries nothing more than a puppet; he was indeed nominally the first prince in the land, but actually he remained a tool in the hands of the Shogun: surrounded by his troops, and, under pretence of guarding his person, kept in complete seclusion. The dynasty of the Shoguns was hereditary, in the same way as was that of the Mikado; and we are here concerned

---

[1] *Lit.* 'Great Prince.'
[2] *Lit.* ' Barbarian-suppressing Commander-in-Chief.'

with the most famous, and the last, of these Shogun dynasties, bearing the family name of Tokugawa. To these potentates are erected the splendid monumental temples which every traveller visits and admires. All dynasties must have an end, all kingdoms rise and fall in due rotation; but when one reads about these fine old soldiers and statesmen, their reign of two hundred and fifty years, during which peace and prosperity blessed the land, it comes almost as a painful shock to find that all was brought to an abrupt end by anything so intensely new and, one almost feels, incongruous as Commodore Perry and an American man-o'-war.

At Nikko, later, we shall come to the tomb of the first Shogun, the great general Ieyasu, founder of the dynasty. Here on the borders of the beautiful Shiba Park, in Tokyo, we find the mausolea of no less than six of his successors in the title, including the fourteenth, who died in 1866. The fifteenth and last of the Shoguns still lives at Shizuoka in Suruga, bereft of his power, a vassal where he was chief of all.

In Ueno Park, another beautiful spot in Tokyo, rest six more Shoguns. And at Nikko, close to the celebrated founder of his race, lies one Shogun, the third of the line. That completes the list, and to each of them is erected a mausoleum in itself a complete work of art—national monuments of priceless value untouched by the hand of decay, buried amidst colossal trees, the brilliant memorials of Old Japan.

Thinking over this great past, a feeling almost of resentment arises within one against the 'agent of a brand-new civilisation.' Old Japan is disappearing fast, and the New Japan seems in danger of becoming the Ramsgate and Margate of the American population. To hear a Carson City counter-jumper expatiating on his exalted position as a 'free-born 'Merukun citizen' under the shadow of the tomb of the first Shogun brings ancient dignity and modern vulgarity into sufficiently strong contrast. Most travellers would perhaps rather be spared the contrast.

But to return to the temples of Tokyo. To those that have not a gift in that direction, the visiting of temple after temple becomes far more of a toil than a pleasure. It is like 'doing' the endless picture-galleries of Europe in a hurry. Not only do we fail to appreciate the beauties of each picture, but they all become blended into one miserable whole—inseparably connected with a feeling of sore feet and an aching back. Therefore, perhaps, it is wise for ordinary mortals to visit only the best temples, and to make a very leisurely and restful business of this. At Tokyo the finest is that of the second Shogun in Shiba Park; and a quiet morning or afternoon spent here will give a very fair idea of the general character and style of architecture and decoration, employed on a less magnificent scale in the others.

In Ueno Park is a fine museum, a modern building, and a small zoological garden containing nothing of any particular interest. In the museum is the state bullock-cart which was used by the old Mikados—a huge vehicle in which his Imperial Majesty sat half-shrouded from the public gaze. Amidst cases of old armour and Japanese antiquities, you come suddenly across a case containing a collection of Christian relics. Some of these were represented by the Pope to the Japanese mission which visited his court 280 years ago, and include a picture of our Saviour with the crown of thorns on his head. Alongside are the 'trampling boards,' oblong metal blocks on which are embossed scriptural scenes connected with the death of our Lord. On these boards all suspected of Christianity were compelled to trample as an open token of apostasy. The Dutch traders are reported to have acquiesced in this practice rather than abandon their trading business in the country.

To those who are in search of unique and picturesque country scenes, in the vicinity of Tokyo, can be recommended a drive to the iris garden of Horikiri. The irises are in full bloom in June, whilst earlier in the year the drive will take you through endless avenues of cherry-trees in full blossom. At Horikiri is a very picturesque tea-house: summer-houses, dwarf trees, and pretty little waitresses, all complete. The rickshaw drive occupies one and a quarter hours each way, and at least two men per rickshaw are required.

Wonderful fellows, these rickshaw men, and of surprising speed and endurance. To run sixteen miles in a hot sun, drawing a rickshaw, even on the flat, is no mean performance. And on top of that to be ready for another long job in the afternoon speaks volumes in favour of the hardy little Titan. The wage in Tokyo is 75 cents a day.

Whilst we were there, all the city was in a *furore* over the expected arrival of Lieut.-Colonel Fukushima, the Japanese officer who rode from Berlin to the western coast of China in sixteen months. The Japanese high and low were jubilant over the feat of their countryman; and a grand public reception, with triumphal arches, was accorded him on the racecourse. The ride was made for a wager, which the Colonel unhappily lost, for the ride was to be completed in twelve months, and only one horse was to be ridden throughout. Three horses were found necessary, and he was four months overdue.

CHAPTER IX

THE COOL SHADES OF NIKKO

TOWARDS the end of June we found Tokyo getting unpleasantly warm, and the cooling shades of Nikko as portrayed in the beautiful photographs to be purchased waved an irresistible welcome.

The journey occupies about five hours, the distance being eighty miles. Not very rapid travelling this, but a strict regard to economy in working the line forbids an increase of pace. The first-class carriages are very comfortable, being exact miniatures of the carriages of Indian railways, and what in England would be called saloon carriages. The second-class is also very good: generally two long seats facing each other running down the length of the carriage, as in the interior of an omnibus. The fares are very moderate, being 3 cents (about a penny) a mile first-class, 2 cents a mile second-class, and

1 cent a mile third-class. A free allowance of luggage is allowed in the proportion of 140 lbs. to a first-class passenger, 88 lbs. to a second-class, and 40 lbs. to a third-class. Practically any amount of luggage, within reason, is allowed to a first-class passenger. The system of registration is employed as in India, but in a much simpler form. There are, for each package, two numbered metallic discs, one of which is tied to the trunk and one is given to the owner. At the end of the journey the checks are handed in and the luggage recovered.

There are no refreshment-rooms, with European food, at any of the stations; therefore provender for the way should be taken. All the hotels are well up in this portion of a traveller's comfort, and make up enticing little baskets for the journey. Japanese tea can be bought at some stations for about a penny; *this includes the teapot and teacup*, which remain with the purchaser.

At the Arai Hotel at Nikko we gained our first experience of a Japanese hotel owned and managed by a Japanese: and a very pleasing experience it was. The proprietor caters for both foreigners and his own countrymen; and in one portion of the hotel the rooms are Japanese fashion, and in the other European fashion, both being spick-and-span and as clean as a thrifty housemaid can make them. As we approach, a hurry and bustle about the portico is visible, and when we reach it two rows of merry little ladies all bows and smiles, and a sprinkling of men, with the proprietor, all help us to alight, who fuss about as if one of the most important events in history was just happening. 'Will this room suit your Excellency, or this, or that?' And with many bows and polite speeches we are shown over the house. The charge is $2\frac{1}{2}$ to 3 dollars a head a day, or 90 dollars a month. This includes everything. Hot baths all day and every day, lights, attendance, boots, three square meals, besides early breakfast (the *chota-hazri* of the East), also afternoon tea. The *cuisine* at this hotel was excellent—not thereby meaning excellent only when compared to what one would expect in a small country inn, but really first-rate. The cook had evidently been highly trained by a European in all the more delicate *minutiæ* of his art, whilst the solid joys of the table were amply represented by the best salmon and salmon-trout, admirable beef, and first-class poultry. The beers and wines were very good, and the prices lower than we pay at an hotel in England. For instance, table claret from Bordeaux is charged at 1s. 4d. only a quart. Moët and Chandon champagne, 8s.; Hiedsieck's Dry Monopole, 9s. 4d.; beer, 8d.; and so on. Anything more kind and obliging than the attendance it is impossible to have. It always seemed to be the height of enjoyment to every one to serve us in every way; and never were we caught out in a shower without the whole countryside being scoured by people bringing us umbrellas and waterproofs.

One diminutive person took us completely under her dominion, and administered with elaborate care to our wants. Her English was quaint and rather elementary; amongst other things, she insisted on calling the canary 'a leetle cheekin.' The son of the proprietor, fairly well versed in English, carried on the correspondence part of the business, and he often came to me to have his letters corrected before posting them. These often caused us much amusement, but the seal of confession precludes their publication. One day, however, I chanced across the young man with the root of all his learning before him—a *Polite Letter Writer*. The *Polite Letter Writer* is public property, therefore there is no necessity for concealing its contents. My young friend, being anxious to order up some wines and stores from Yokohama, naturally took to his book. In 'ordering goods' the *Letter Writer* gave him the following useful lead: 'Gentlemen (or Dear Sirs), I will thank you to purchase for my account 200 bales fair Oomrawuttee cotton, at the market price, on receipt of this, unless otherwise advised by wire, and ship the same by a vessel classed A1 at Lloyd's, affecting insurance thereon as heretofore.' We can imagine the heartrending struggles of a foreigner in endeavouring to transpose this to suit his case, and the highly ludicrous result when the letter was accomplished.

Again, a lady who had been at the hotel before wrote asking about rooms. Out comes the *Polite Writer*. Here we are—the very thing! 'From a Gentleman to a Lady whom he has met only once.' Met once before—most appropriate! Needless to say, the letter is a highly erotic effusion ending : ' Pleading your beauty and grace of person, and charms of manner and mind, as my excuse for venturing to write to you, I remain, Madam, etc.' As may be imagined, this made a very telling and effective ending to the reply about the rooms.

Now, I am not going to bore people in general with descriptions of temples about which they know nothing and possibly care less—which they will never see, and have not the remotest wish to see. The select few who 'know all about it' will find pages and pages on the subject which have been written by other people who also know all about it. To them for regular information let the student of architecture and Buddhist lore refer. At the same time, let me plead guilty, for once in a way, to entering on a subject about which my knowledge is of the feeblest. Let my apology be, that probably no man, or woman, can visit the great mausoleum of the first Shogun, at Nikko, without feeling irresistibly moved to expatiate on the subject afterwards. This shall be my sole transgression. Other temples may be mentioned, in a cursory way; but their description shall, with all deference, be left to more competent pens.

A little history to start with. It has before been explained that a Shogun was a great military ruler nominally subservient to the Mikado, but in reality ruling him and his people with a rod of iron, or, perhaps more accurately, with a sword of the best steel. The greatest of these was the founder of the last dynasty of Shoguns. His name was Ieyasu, and he is generally called the first Shogun, though as a matter of fact the Shogunate had existed for four hundred years before his time. A fine fellow

A SAMURAI (THE FIGHTING CLASS)

this, and a great soldier; not only a great soldier, though, but a great statesman as well. A man of good family, and at the same time a soldier of fortune, at the age of forty-eight he defeated the combined forces of his opponents in Japan at the great battle of Seki-ga-hara, and three years later obtained from the Mikado the title of Shogun. Having secured this kingly position with the sword, he set to work, like a great and far-seeing mind, to consolidate his power and to secure the succession to his descendants, by solid and statesmanlike legislation. The proof of the greatness of any man's prescience lies in the future. Two hundred and fifty years of peace and prosperity stand as a monumental proof of Ieyasu's greatness. His statecraft, like many other great and successful things, was simplicity itself. On the pretext of guarding the sanctity of the Mikado, he placed his person under the strictest military surveillance. The great feudal lords, the daimios, he played off one against another, whilst he secured to himself a predominating influence in their disputes by seizing, and annexing to his family possessions, strategic points in all parts of the country. These points his unerring military genius detected as being dominant positions in any important dispute. Two hundred and fifty years demonstrated the commanding value of these positions; and their inviolability was further secured by the provisions of a law which till quite recently made it a capital offence to enter any property of the Shogun without leave. Death by crucifixion was the penalty exacted. Ieyasu was born A.D. 1552, and died A.D. 1616. And now to his tomb and mausoleum.

THE TOMB OF A GREAT SOLDIER

CHAPTER X

THE TOMB OF A GREAT SOLDIER

On the cool hillside, approached by a broad gravel path and a flight of stone steps, imbedded amidst ancient trees, lie the bones of the greatest soldier and statesman whom Japan has produced. The tomb itself is solid simplicity: a miniature bronze pagoda before which stands a large bronze stork holding a candlestick. Around runs a stone wall and balustrade, through which a bronze gateway gives access to the tomb. But in sharp contrast to the simple tomb lie below mausolea and shrines gorgeous beyond description, enamelled with gold and red, richly carved, and highly decorated. These memorial buildings take the form of one large main building, of the usual shape of Japanese temples; and this is approached through a series of courtyards, each one above the other, and each containing smaller buildings of great richness and variety. The gateways which lead from one court to another are also of the richest designs, and beautifully carved.

Approaching the mausoleum from the road below, the first object of interest is a very fine pagoda, red and gold, an offering of affection from a friend and contemporary of the great man. Round the base of this are carved the twelve signs of the zodiac. These are described by enthusiasts as 'lifelike.' Perhaps it is open to question whether any carving can strictly be called lifelike when it takes some little consideration to decide whether the object represented is a rat or a sheep. Perhaps more harm than good is done to ancient Japanese art by overrating it. Let us ordinary, uninspired travellers at once confess that, beautiful and gorgeous and interesting though they are, it is impossible to compare for a moment the best Japanese mausolea with the *chef-d'œuvres* of Europe, or of India, or of China.

There is nothing in Japan to compare

with the Taj at Agra, for instance, or the Cathedral at Milan. Yet is the work often excellent, and only seems indifferent to those who have been taught to expect too great things of it.

Passing through the first gateway, a courtyard is entered in which are to be seen several objects of interest. To the right are three fair-sized buildings, handsomely decorated, and used as storehouses for the relics of Ieyasu—his furniture, pictures, and other treasures. Here also are deposited the paraphernalia which are used in the commemorative processions which take place annually on June 1st. We were specially fortunate in chancing upon a unique scene here. A Japanese amateur photographer, evidently a gentleman of considerable influence, had procured the ancient robes of the Shogun and his train of nobles. His friends, dressed in these, were arranged in procession up the steps leading to the main shrine. As we entered the courtyard the camera was hid from us, and we walked straight in to a scene 200 years old, with all its actual surroundings. The camera was the largest we had ever seen, the plate measuring 36 inches by 30 inches. Watching the scene, we found we were leaning against a paling which surrounds a stately tree. This tree, according to tradition, Ieyasu used to carry about as an ornament in his litter, when it was small enough to go into a flower-pot. A couple of yards off is the stall wherein is stabled the sacred pony, an albino, at this moment out grazing. A velvet-covered headstall and—gracious heavens! is it possible?—a common whip hang on the wall. This pony is led near the head of the procession, as shown in the engraving, and is kept for the use of the god. Round the walls of the stable on the outside are groups of monkeys carved in high-relief, life-size. Amongst these is a group of three: the monkeys of India, China, and Japan. One is represented shading his eyes, the second closing his mouth, and the third shutting his ears. They are allegorical representations of three great virtues. They see no wrong, they hear no wrong, and they speak no wrong. We might introduce this trio into Europe. A little further on in this courtyard is the solid grey granite trough of holy water in which the faithful, on payment of a small fee, may purify themselves before proceeding. We noticed that, though many threw a copper to the attendant, comparatively few accepted the proffered ladle of water. Close to the trough is another fine building, in which is to be found a revolving bookcase containing the Buddhist scriptures, as at Asakusa; but the vulgar are not here allowed to turn it.

In the next courtyard above are to be seen, on payment of a small fee, in a corridor, many relics of the Shogun: his litter, dresses, several swords, helmets, and very good pictures of hawks—hawking being his favourite pastime. At the other extremity of this court is a sacred dancing-shed, in which is seated a lady—well, no longer young—clad in a scarlet skirt, and with a white cap on her head somewhat like that of a Norman peasant. Any one who expects anything volatile or frivolous is, on the face of it, bound to be disappointed. For ten cents the lady kindly consented to perform, and we came to the conclusion that it was ten cents very easily earned. The dance consisted of walking slowly and demurely to the front of the stage, shaking a large rattle three or four times with one hand, and then a fan three or four times with the other. Then right-about turn, and a demure retirement to the back of the shed. The same simple manœuvre is executed over and over again, as long as one cares to stop and see it. When all other trades fail, I am thinking of setting up as a sacred dancer myself.

Some time after writing this account of the sacred dance, I came across the following description of the same artiste's performance by a very distinguished author:—'Our guide threw a coin into the box in front of her. Upon this she rose, and with extremely becoming movements commenced the *kagura*, or temple dance, beating slow time to her own steps with the bunch of silver bells held in her right hand, and waving her fan to the same cadence with her left, while performing what was a most rhythmical, solemn, and striking *pas seul.* Her white head-dress, almost Abyssinian in style, her large white sleeves and scarlet *obi*, made her very pictorial; and she was besides this so entirely comely, gentle, and demure, that when she bowed her head, closed her fan, and sank back again into dreamy silence, I asked my interpreter what gift he had made for so delightful a little ceremony.' It had been about twopence—but that is neither here nor there. I merely make the quotation to show with what different eyes two people look on the self-same performance. Certainly, no one can complain of being disappointed in the reality after reading mine.

Again ascending into another courtyard through a very fine gate, we come to the main shrine. Here, as usual, boots are taken off, and, supplied with cotton substitutes, it is permissible to enter alone and study the interior at one's leisure. A large matted room, perfectly empty except for a small shrine, is first entered, the walls and ceilings of which are richly decorated. On the right and left of this large room are two small ones, one of which was reserved for the Shogun's use. It is a very handsome little room, the walls and ceiling of which are elaborately carved. To the rear of the big room, a flight of lacquer steps leads first down and then up to the inner, chapel. Outside, the building is brilliant with gold and red, a sparkling jewel set in the deep green of the forest foliage.

A very lame description this, believe me, of a very beautiful cluster of buildings. Let me ask those who really appreciate Japanese art to borrow, or buy, some book where an expert describes these things. Murray's book, amongst others, is excellent.

Great heavens! I have forgotten the cat. The cat, which every one goes to see in this temple enclosure. It is called the sleeping cat, and is by a famous Japanese artist. We expected to see an animal as large as the Lion of Lucerne, and twice as well executed. The reality is the size of a kitten, and might have dropped straight out of the Lowther

Arcade. Mythical animals the ancient Japanese may have been good at, but certainly not at domestic creatures.

'Nikko is the rainiest place in Japan.' Quite so; our experience confirms that dictum. Out of ten days it poured with astonishing vigour for more than six. There was no necessity to go out long walks to see waterfalls; we had only to sit in the veranda to see a magnificent cascade off the roof. The other days were very bright and warm, the difference of temperature varying between 86° on the warmest day and 70° on the rainiest. A fall of 16° in twenty-four hours takes one straight from the airiest of tropical garments into clothes that are worn on a fairly cold day in England. The sun is quite powerful enough to make a sun-hat welcome, but most people seem to find a straw hat with an umbrella sufficient protection.

As I was inditing these and other highly interesting remarks, a great hullabaloo arose below, accompanied by the barking and yapping of dogs. It appeared that a wild dog had snapped up a small white Maltese terrier, probably in its ignorance mistaking it for a lamb or a rabbit. The terrier was recovered all right, but the incident caused us much amusement by reason of the struggles of a rather stout gentleman to get out of his chair and rush to the rescue. As he explained afterwards, with perfect solemnity, he was sitting 'in one of those infernal chairs which get up with you!' Like many other things in Japan, these chairs are made to fit a small race of beings, and the brawny Briton, unless he makes a slow and dignified withdrawal, is very apt to find his chair 'getting up with him.'

Our little maid every morning got into a tremendous fuss about the baths. Now, there were four bathrooms, and never more than eight people in the hotel, yet she was never happy till she had worked us all off. About seven o'clock she used to begin. 'Bath ready, sir.' 'No, I don't want a bath now; I ordered it at 8.30.' Then she would go off and try all the other seven people, and sometimes,

PREPARING THE BATH

perhaps, catch a newcomer. This was a moment of triumph. He was immediately marched off, put through the mill, and marched back again. Each of us in turn was eventually dragged forth and one by one marched down, the little woman going before with the sponge and towels. Finishing one's bath, she again appeared, trotted in front, opened the bedroom door, put you safely in, and shut it. 'Thank goodness! another of these lazy people finished off for the day!' Finally we all get down, twenty minutes too early for breakfast—and every one knows what that means.

No one who has a few days to spare should fail to spend one of them up at Lake Chuzenji, some 2000 feet above Nikko. The distance is estimated at seven and a half miles, but it takes a good three hours to cover the distance, riding, walking, or rickshawing. A combination of riding and walking is the most comfortable. During this pilgrimage we made our first acquaintance with the Japanese pony. He is rather a good beast in his way, and far superior to the mutton-headed, beefy-shouldered quadruped people risk their lives upon in China. One of the ponies, a four-year-old belonging to the hotel, was really a well-bred mare, and quite the cut of a polo pony, or second-class racing pony. Thirty dollars would have bought her. Prices, they told me, ranged from fifteen to seventy dollars a-head at Nikko. Probably the Yokohama people know their own business best, but it was somewhat of a surprise to see in the papers that the Europeans import ponies from China. They subscribe together, apparently, and buy a batch in China: these are shipped across, and immediately on their arrival lots are drawn for them. About 100 dollars, in the list we saw, was the price the subscriber landed his animal for. That is Rs. 200, or £12, 10s.

The lake is a neat, green, little spot, a regular mountain lake, some 4500 feet above the sea. It is about seven miles long and two miles broad; and all round fine forest trees descend to the water's edge. Fish of several sporting kinds abound, including salmon, salmon-trout, and trout. At the near corner is a small hamlet, with one or two tea-houses, where one may pass the night comfortably enough. We here had the misfortune to meet the prototype of that lodging-house keeper who, sanctified by tradition, still exists at some English watering-places. She charged us the equivalent of two full days' board and lodging for resting an hour and eating a light repast of fish and eggs. To the honour of the Japanese, be it said, these harpies are rare as snowflakes in a summer sky. Whilst on the lake, under the tender care of a gentleman who evidently would have been more at home with a ploughshare than in handling the sail of a boat, we were caught in a regular tropical squall of wind and rain. Earnestly encouraged by us, the bold mariner discreetly lowered the sail, and we rowed home; or rather he rowed, and we put up paper umbrellas and tried to imagine that we were not sitting under the main cataract of Niagara. By no means despicable things, though, these paper umbrellas, in sunshine or as a protection against light showers. They cost about a shilling a-piece, and very pretty and graceful they look. We exported a small cargo of them.

There are only two private houses on the lake; and the whole place, village and all, is deserted in winter, when the lake is frozen nearly solid, and the ice covered deep with snow. Our ever-thoughtful host of the Arai, without orders—and it may be mentioned without extra charge—sent a most enticing little lunch after us by the hand of the groom. Each course, beautifully carved and put together, was fitted into a separate little box: whilst the etceteras, butter, salt, and pepper, each had its own little box. The whole parcel was not more than twelve inches long by six inches deep; yet within that small space was a tasty little lunch for two. Even a couple of picturesque paper napkins, quite little gems in their way, and really much too good to be desecrated, were not forgotten.

It is quite natural that some of the tradespeople should add to my stock of quaint notices. Here is an ambitious person who aspires to French as well as English :

> OSHIMA
>
> CAILLEUR POUR DAMES
>
> ROBES ET MOUTIOUE
>
> *Clothing of woman tailor*

If any lady can explain what a 'moutioue' is, she will infinitely oblige the writer by doing so, either publicly or privately.

It is always refreshing to come across a good, thoroughpaced piece of what is vulgarly called humbug. Busybodies, the Rev. Washington P. Gingham and other highly commendable persons, have impressed upon the Mikado and his advisers the extreme sinfulness, not to speak of the indelicacy, of allowing people to bathe in public in the costume affected by our good ancestors Adam and Eve. Even the rickshaw men have to wear certain prescribed garments.

If the Japanese are so polite and obliging as to abandon their ancient customs out of deference to the prurient mind of the West—we can only commend their pliability. But, having done so, it must be a source of considerable surprise and perplexity to them to find in every little tobacco-shop, in every little village in Japan, packets of American cigarettes, many of which contain pictures, harmless enough, perhaps, but which to ordinary eyes are more indelicate, and even indecent, than bathing in the suit of clothes provided by Nature. I wonder some one has not publicly set up the great god 'Humbug' as a deity of the first water; he has certainly more followers than many of his less fortunate brethren.

We met with our old friend 'Jingo' in Japan, and were surprised to find that she was a lady. The Empress Jingo, a great warrior-queen, ruled over Japan some 1600 years ago. She is credited with having conquered Korea; and her son is to this day worshipped as the God of War, the local Mars. The fine old British song—

> 'We don't want to fight,
> But, by Jingo, if we do,' etc.—

therefore invokes a real deity, and is not merely a music-hall adjuration. This is very comforting.

One of the chief products of Nikko is fur slippers. Here may be found otter, beaver, badger, monkey, wild dog, marten, rabbit, wild cat, and white beaver slippers of every size and shape at a moderate price. For a good otter-skin eight dollars were asked; but probably an all-round price of five dollars a piece would purchase any quantity. Beaver and badger were about equal value, and were priced somewhat lower than otter. The other furs were cheaper, some indeed costing as low as 50 cents for a pair of slippers.

Our handmaid, ever obliging, cut out and helped to make up a Japanese dressing-gown. Completed, the garment cost about $1.25; and very pretty and effective it was. Perhaps it would not be out of place to recommend travellers who want the real Japanese article to do the same. The silk-shops of Yokohama are full of dressing-gowns of every material and pattern; but these are expressly made for us foreigners, and are generally not such as are worn by the people. To be assured of getting the real thing it is wiser to buy any pretty materials one comes across, and to have them made up by any Japanese tailor or seamstress, for all are accustomed to make these clothes. No respectable Japanese lady after the age of twenty-one wears any but the most subdued colours—dove-colour and French grey predominating. The bright colours and bright patterns are left for younger folks.

The Nikko valley, as far as scenery goes, might be almost anywhere—North Wales, Scotland, Hungary, Switzerland. In fact, a deep wooded glen with a fine, tumbling, mountain torrent flowing through it : a wonderfully beautiful little spot, and possessing one scenic charm which the others have not, namely, the avenues of giant cryptomerias. Those not pressed for time can here spend a restful, enjoyable, and comfortable month, very economically.

CHAPTER XI

HOT SPRINGS IN THE HILLS

Our next sojourn was at Ikao, only some fifty miles as the crow flies from Nikko, but a laborious day's journey round by train, tram, and rickshaw. Some prefer to travel across the hills by road all the way; but it is a rough journey, suitable only for the hardy pedestrian, and not to be commended where ladies are concerned. From door to door our journey occupied thirteen hours: seven and a half hours by train, one and a half by tram, and two and a half by rickshaw; the balance being made up by various necessary detentions. From Maebashi, the railway terminus, to Ikao is practically one long pull of fifteen miles up hill: hence the extreme tedium. Moreover, the rickshaw men here seemed to be short of work, and in very bad training compared to those elsewhere. At Maebashi station we met with most handsome and courteous treatment at the hands of the stationmaster. Our host of the Arai had written him a short note asking him to give us a helping-hand, and in response he immediately and decisively took us in charge. He cleared our baggage, procured rickshaws, drove a mile with us to the tram terminus, took our tickets, engaged a special car, impressed upon the conductor many parting injunctions, and with profuse bows backed himself away, without even allowing us to pay his rickshaw fare.

Into a special tramcar, which only costs $2.50, you can take all your baggage, and as many people as can be squeezed in. A rickshaw carries from 80lbs. to 100lbs. of baggage. Very wearily we arrived at Ikao, at about 8 P.M.; for a short journey which takes a long time always seems infinitely more tiring than a long journey which occupies the same time. At the hotel here we had a magnificent view from our rooms; but that was all we had to live upon. The food was pretentious but poor, and the attendance—well, there was none. It is always a difficult matter recommending hotels, for they vary much from year to year. This hotel is highly recommended by several writers, and in Murray's *Guide* is honoured with an asterisk denoting especial excellence. Yet it is now much inferior to its rivals. On the other hand, the Arai at Nikko, which we found so comfortable, is not mentioned at all. But what is excellent this year might another year be exceedingly uncomfortable. At present a *cordon bleu*, late of the British Embassy, superintends the *cuisine* there; next year he may have flown. Some people say that, apart from the cooking, hotels deteriorate from contamination with foreign travellers, unaccustomed to the usages of the East. To the free-born 'Merukun, who is everlastingly booming bad English and the Stars and Stripes into every stray stranger, it appears inconceivably degrading for any person to bow down before him. Are we not all men and brothers?—excluding, of course, the heathen Chinee — and why should one grovel before another? Such oracular declarations, quite commonly to be heard, are founded on a somewhat imperfect conception of what is debasing and what is not. To bow down to the ground is no more debasing to a Japanese than it is for you or me to take off our hats. The act is one merely of courtesy or respect. In old-fashioned hotels crowds of handy, cheerful little maids, with the deepest respect and the most delightful alacrity, minister to one's wants. In the new-fashioned hotels, careless, ignorant women, who have lost all their Japanese ways and manners, leave one's room uncleaned and one's bed unmade, to smoke pipes and gossip downstairs. The very scantiest courtesy, and, what is more important, scantiest attendance, do they bestow on any one. A deterioration due to whom? Undoubtedly to foreigners. When we hear an American gentleman, in the hall of an hotel, with delicate irony asking one of the girls why she 'don't stand on her head' while she is about it, we can hardly blame that girl for not bowing to the next stranger with equal politeness. Once remove the outward form of respect, and with all Eastern nations deterioration in manners immediately sets in.

In all the hotels, and in many of the houses at Ikao, hot mineral-water baths form part of the establishment. The water is 115° Fahrenheit, and at our hotel flowed into square baths, their tops flush with the floor, measuring 8 ft. × 3 ft. × 2 ft. These baths are divided one from another, and the natural water flows through them day and night. At any moment one can drop in, and find everything ready. Sulphate of soda and iron are the minerals, but very slightly diluted. The water is supposed to be specially efficacious in cases of rheumatism. The beds of the streams in this region become bright yellow from the action of this water, and the people of the place drive a thriving trade in cotton goods dyed a natural yellow by merely pegging them down in the stream. These cottons are considered extremely strengthening when wrapped about the loins. Much ingenuity is displayed in the variety of patterns this nature dye is led to make. We bought some dressing-gowns, one covered with bamboo leaves, another with storks, and another with fishes. The dye is perfectly fast, and nothing will wash it out.

Above Ikao is the bijou lake of Haruna. At Nikko, and round the lake above it, the country is densely wooded; but here the whole country has the appearance of immense moors covered with bracken, long grass, and low bushes. The views are therefore unobstructed, and are probably unsurpassed in all Japan for breadth and beauty. Haruna Lake is about a couple of hours' walk from Ikao, and a stiffish climb for half the way. The lake is about a mile across at its broadest part: it is surrounded by quaint peaks a few hundred feet high— one being a miniature Mount Fuji. Beyond the lake you can drop down, a mile or more, to a quaint old Shinto temple, so placed as to be beneath a huge boulder, which without a shadow of a doubt will make pulp of the priest the next time an earthquake passes that way. We had a coolie who carried our lunch and showed us the way. He was like an old cab-horse in London—one of those which stops automatically at all the public-houses. Tea was our man's beverage, and it required eight separate doses of it to get him through the job. At lunch he indiscreetly indulged in a glass of saké, the native liquor, and evidently had a mouth like an apple-tree all the way home from the effects of it. At the lake is a rough dairy-farm, where excellent milk can be procured. Fish are supposed to abound; but during a week's stay at Ikao we only had one kind, and that an inferior trout. Either no one knows how to catch them, or else they are not there.

A little English girl in the hotel took me for a long walk down to Benten-daki, a very pretty waterfall in the valley below. Before we had gone two yards she had said, 'Now, tell me some stories about snakes—*horrible* ones.' I unwound about a mile and a half of the most blood-curdling snake stories that imagination would supply. We then got on to tigers, then leopards, and finally descended to wild bulls, wolves, and the most harrowing species of battle stories. That brought us to the waterfall, and tea, and peace generally. A nice, fresh little girl, who should grow up into a fresh and clever little woman.

They sell here neat little camp-stools, which, instead of being used as seats, are used as pillows. They fold quite flat, and are invaluable for the midday snooze at the midday tea-house. It was at this hotel our first experience of regular Japanese rooms with paper walls. The experience is somewhat startling at first, but one gets accustomed to it. Every word and sound is of course distinctly audible from room to room, and as often as not the indiscreet corner of a box, or an inquisitive finger, has made one's abode a palace of glass. The signal for calling a servant is to clap your hands. You might clap the hands for a month in a stone house without attracting any attention. Here you can lie in bed and clap your hands, and the sound is audible in the remotest corner of the servants' quarters. When we read that the Shoguns of old, as part of their system, reduced espionage to a fine art, we can imagine how much simplified the matter became for the spies, when with the point of the finger easy acoustic—and ocular—supervision could be exercised over nearly every house in the town.

The people of Japan wear sandals or clogs, one thong of which passes between the great toe and its neighbour. One of our acquaintances here was educating his toes up to this high ideal by wearing corks between them! In comparing Ikao with other Japanese hill resorts, it may be noted in its favour that it is cool and open, with wide expansive views uninterrupted by dense foliage or cramped by near hills. The mineral baths are strengthening and invigorating; and the hotels, though not very comfortable, are remarkably cheap. Our hotel bill for two persons, including wine, came to $38 only for one week.

CHAPTER XII

THE LAKE DISTRICT OF HAKONÉ

IT may be useful to remember that a telegram worded in English is a very expensive luxury, whereas the same information may be transmitted in Japanese for a trifle. The managers of hotels are always ready to wire in the vernacular for a foreigner.

The address counts as part of the telegram in English, but not in Japanese. Postage is 2 cents for an ordinary letter, and 10 cents for letters to England or India. It must be remembered that, though the postal service is well organised, letters do not travel very fast; and therefore, in writing on matters which require an answer, due allowance should be made. This was brought home to us at one place at which, though it was situated on the railway, it took the best part of ten days to get some money from Yokohama. The distance was only eighty miles or so, and therefore a simple mathematical calculation will show that it was possible to have walked to the bank and back in that time. Japan is not the only place, however, where letters travel slowly, if surely. From my regimental headquarters in India it is possible —and not only possible but perfectly easy, for the feat has repeatedly been accomplished—to post a letter to Nowshera, fifteen miles distant, on Monday, and not to get the answer till Thursday. In the same way the daily paper takes eighteen hours traversing the same distance. These are glorious realities.

In travelling by train in Japan, we were recommended to go first-class, as the habits of the middle-class Japanese were stated to be not always such as a lady might approve of. Accident introduced us to the second-class, and we were very agreeably surprised with it. On one train all the first-class was full, on the next the same, and on the third there were no first-class carriages. We had first-class tickets for these three, and had to travel second-class. After that we took second-class tickets, and moved into the first-class if it were necessary. As to the company, we preferred that of the second-class, for one does not come to Japan to be boxed up perpetually with parties of foreign tourists. As to the habits of the Japanese, the only one that was at all offensive was the expectoral activity of a small minority. To any one who has experienced the steady persistency of the Yankee in this respect, or has met the Frenchman in his native carriage, the experience, though disagreeable, will be nothing new. In all other respects we found our fellow-travellers clean, obliging, and the acme of good-nature. Pecuniarily, with heavy baggage, for which extra charge is made, the saving is infinitesimal. Lightly equipped, an economy of one-third is effected.

Railway travelling in July we found somewhat sultry work, the thermometer registering as high as 92°, and the carriages being fairly full all along. Our destination being the popular baths of Mujanoshita, we found that it was necessary to break the journey, and did so accordingly at the Imperial Hotel, Tokyo. This is really a first-class hotel, and would do credit to the sea front at Brighton. Why don't they have hotels like this in India? Next day a journey of six hours by train, tram, and rickshaw brought us to our destination. Though refreshment-rooms are conspicuous by their absence, yet at many stations trays of very good confectionery, sponge-cakes and the like, are handed along: whilst for drink, bottled beer, tea, and lemonade are obtainable. To us a new and very excellent drink recommended itself. It consists of a tumbler of grated ice, into which is put a squeeze of lemon, half a bottle of lemonade, or a dash of whisky. On a hot day a great number of these doses may be applied to the person, with eminently gratifying results. The machine on which the ice is shaved is like an inverted carpenter's plane.

The much-lauded Mujanoshita we were

disappointed with. The hotel, which was described as the best in Japan, we found only moderate; the scenery insignificant compared to other places; and the whole place swarmed with Americans and Europeans. On the morning of our arrival there were forty-four at our hotel: nineteen left that day, and more streamed in in their places. The redeeming feature is the water; it is like velvet, and makes bathing more than ever a luxury. Here, for the sum of $3, we bought quite a gem of a luncheon-box—*bento* (box) in the Japanese tongue. It stands a foot high and six inches square, lacquer and bamboo work throughout, and very light. In this small space an ample and appetising lunch, with cigars for two people, can be comfortably packed.

Two days of Mujanoshita sufficed us, and then we pushed on up the hill to the beautiful little mountain lake of Hakoné, five miles distant. Here we are in Japan again: leave our boots in the street, live in paper rooms, dine in the veranda on the lake, with the

OUR HOTEL AT HAKONÉ

great Mount Fuji, snow-clad, towering in the distance, and generally enjoy the change from strict civilisation. There are two small villages at the head of the lake, about a mile apart, in which accommodation can generally be found. Some Europeans hire a whole house, and bring their servants with them. Large flocks of sunburnt little boys and girls, in sailor suits, generally form a portion of these households; and thoroughly they seem to enjoy themselves boating, fishing, and bathing all day.

Any ambitious person who wishes to be thoroughly cooked, and to smell a very horrible smell, cannot do better than climb up to Ojigoku, or 'hell's caldron.' We essayed this expedition, expecting to find a veritable caldron, a seething mass of liquid fire, emitting sulphurous flames and smoke —something that might have served as an inspiration to Doré, when illustrating Hell scenes from Dante. After an hour's exceedingly hot climb up an exceedingly steep hill, we came to the desolate top : here, from fissures in the rocky ravines, issue puffs of steam of evil smell. We did not think them worth the climb.

In the little village below, and within view of the lake, are sulphur baths, supplied by the 'hell's caldron' above. Here we lunched at a clean little inn, and here we came across Adam and Eve in their pristine costumes. One old lady especially amused us, for, sublimely regardless of her own absence of clothes, she was transfixed with admiration for my leather gaiters. *Honi soit qui mal y pense*, say I : why on earth should we meddlesome Westerns trouble a guileless villager with our, as likely as not, false notions of decency? Adam and Eve were very happy and comfortable till the serpent arrived and inaugurated the era of top-hats and bombazeen gowns. I see no reason why we should hand on our heritage of woe and clothes to people who are perfectly happy without them. In this connection the Zulu maiden always occurs to me as a case in point. As long as she goes about dressed in nothing at all, she is, without exception, the most virtuous woman in the world. But the moment you make a Christian of her, and put a print frock and flowery hat on her, she becomes the least virtuous and the most degraded of her sex. It is in some quarters considered only a little lower than direct sacrilege to criticise missionaries and their work. Perhaps, however, it is permissible to say that there are missionaries and missionaries. There are some who leave home and wealth, father and mother, relations and friends, and live their lives in pestilential holes: a splendid, manly struggle to do good by example. The highest honour to these. There are others who leave squalour and hard manual or clerical labour in overcrowded cities to live at ease, and in comparative luxury, in sunny lands and amongst a bright and intellectual people. They leave poverty for comparative affluence; they are the well-paid servants of the benevolent public. On purely commercial principles the work of these latter is open to the most searching criticism. I would not for the world, even if competent, enter on such criticism. 'Hell's caldron' specially warmed up for the occasion would be considered much too good a place for the luckless critic. But talking of these enterprises reminds me of a characteristic incident in England. It was the farewell sermon of a young curate who was leaving the parish to go abroad as a missionary. He was quite a young fellow, and preached a most touching sermon: all the old, and some of the young, ladies wept copiously. An honest young parson, without doubt, who firmly believed he was on his way to an honourable martyrdom. The collection was for his benefit, and reached £200! I happened to have personal cognisance of the exact spot he was going to. I knew that his pay was four times higher and his work four times less than in England. And, from personal experience, I knew that the place he was going to was as safe as the pulpit he preached from. If I had made these facts known to the benevolent people who provided £200 for the young parson's outfit, should I have been scoffed at as a heathenish unbeliever or not? My blood curdles at the bare thought.

On the road we met a little group of foster-mothers. The sight is common enough in Japan, the last-born being bound to the back of his little sister. That the last-born does not dislocate his neck, whilst sleeping in this position, is always a source of wonder.

Like most beautiful lakes, that of Hakoné is eminently suitable for philandering and spending a thoroughly lazy time. Is anything more enjoyable, on a bright, warm day, than taking lunch and tea, books, lots of cushions, innumerable cigars, fishing-rods, and departing on the water for the day? A Japanese junk, or sampan, is commodiousness deified: there is room enough to have a small dance on board, therefore comfort is assured. Reclining Cleopatra-like in this happy bark, we are propelled by two willing slaves, working, like a pair of gondoliers, from a position in the stern. Arrived at some shady nook, we anchor, sink all the drinks by strings to the coldest depths, and set to work to fish. The fish are inexperienced and confiding, though small, and fall a ready prey to the inexpert angler. As the day gets warmer the fish go to bed, and won't be disturbed even by a stout worm : a favourable time has arrived for the human lunch. Then a few cigars, an entertaining book, perchance a snooze, till tea-time. By this time the fish are out and about again, and the guileful gondolier, knowing all the most frequented spots, enables us to make up quite a respectable basket before moonrise. Most enjoyable, these days.

The fish in Hakoné lake do not equal, either in quality or in quantity, those caught in the lake above Nikko. Those we caught were a species of lake-trout—very good eating, but there was very little of them. We only came across one small salmon-trout during our stay. The natives resort to netting for all big fish; we saw not a fly-rod on the lake.

Coming home one evening, we heard, across the water, the dulcet strains of 'Ye banks and braes o' bonnie Doon,' sung by many manly throats. Imagine our surprise when we discovered that the throats belonged to a large party of Japanese soldiers in a boat!

A week was all we could spare at this snug little spot. The *kago* (pronounced 'cargo') is at the door, the coolies are portioning out the baggage and drawing lots for the honour and glory of carrying 'their excellencies,' and our host is scrubbing his nose on the floor whilst presenting his bill. This document is about three feet long by eight inches broad, and looks extremely formidable. Out of this mountain of documentary evidence happily emerges a mere mouse of an account, totalling only $40. In this is included board, lodging, beer, wine, waters, and boat-hire for two people for a week. A *kago*, as will be seen from the picture, is exactly made to fit a little Japanese lady, who measures about 4 ft. 10 in. in height. To introduce an ordinary European into the same space is like fitting a cannon-ball into a pill-box. Our journey lay across the hills, to the south-west, from Hakoné lake, and our objective was the Tokaido Railway, at the town of Numadzu.

CHAPTER XIII

THE ABORIGINAL INN

As this chapter will contain our chief experiences of Japanese inns pure and simple, it is hereby dedicated to them. Our way lay along the hoary old paved road, called the Tokaido, which runs from Tokyo to Kyoto—from the capital of the grand old military dictators to the capital of their liege lord, the Mikado. Year by year, for centuries, these old kings of the sword wended their stately way over the abominable paving-stones, a distance of 329 miles each way. Nominally they went to do yearly homage to the divine Mikado: in reality to see that he was kept safe under lock and key, and never so much as touched the ground with his sacred feet.[1] For their own sake it is to be earnestly hoped that the

[1] To carry this idea to its full extent, the Mikado's praying platform was daily strewn with earth, so that he might pray on earth without descending to the earth.

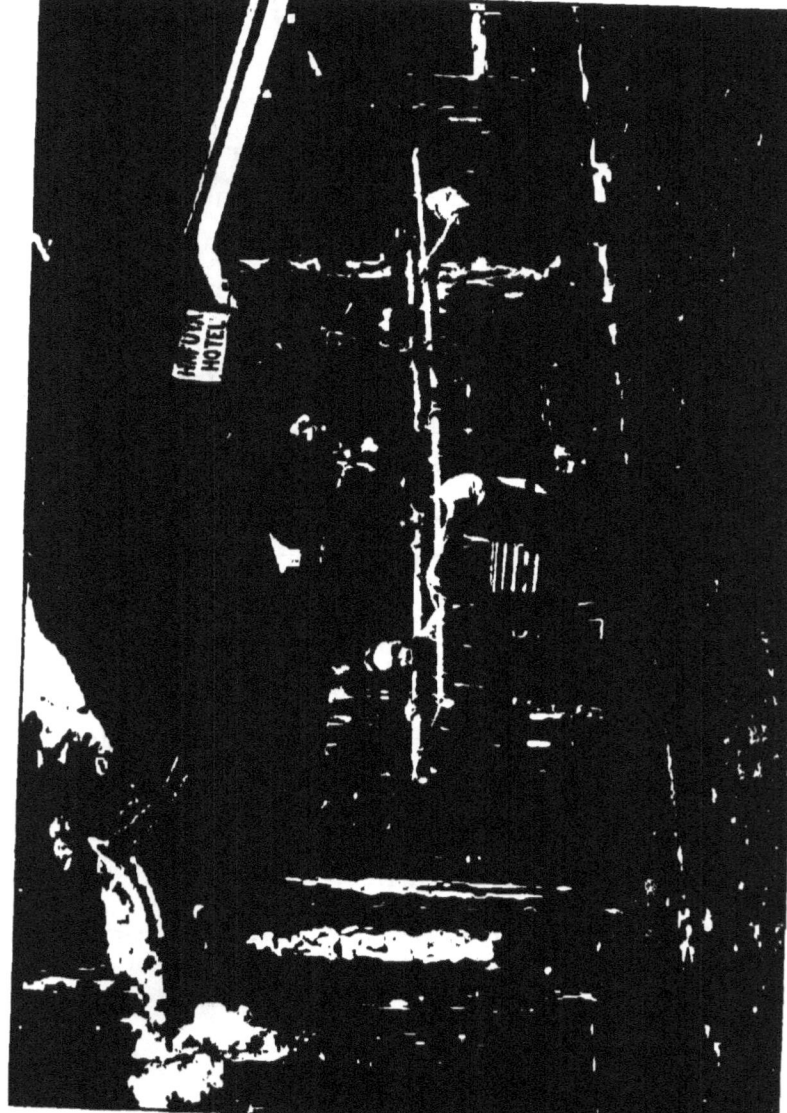

old warriors had something larger than a *kago* to ride in. A horse must be highly unsafe down most of the hills; and to walk is only a little less dangerous. But, putting aside *kagos* and paving-stones, the views during the first few miles from Hakoné are well worth a little tribulation. It is very much easier, too, looking at views going down hill than toiling up. Every yard of the road the traveller can enjoy a prospect which includes sea and land, mountains and plains, rivers and forests. A nice breeze is blowing, and the weather is just pleasant for walking. My *kago* men considered me a most magnificent bargain, for only during a short spell in the day's march did I trouble them. Toiling up the steep hills many men and pack-ponies passed; the latter, like their masters, shod with grass sandals, to prevent their slipping on the knobbly pavement. There must be a great trade in grass sandals, judging from the number of cast-off ones which we found strewed along the road. In one part we counted 133 within the distance of one mile. Using the useful, and wholly reliable, class of statistics so much in favour amongst civilised nations, it will be at once apparent that on this basis 43,757 grass shoes lie on the road between Tokyo and Kyoto. This is a most satisfactory state of affairs —for the shoemakers. Let us go a step further and say, for the State. Here is a fine field for taxation—say a farthing on each pair. The financial prospect is entrancing. New men-of-war would rise like magic from the ashes of a holocaust of sandals.

He is a wonderful little fellow, the rickshaw, or *kago*, man, with an extraordinary partiality for tea. They say that like the willing horse he works too hard, and that pulmonary diseases are making vast strides amongst these indomitable people. It is authoritatively stated that the life of a rickshaw man is but half the life of his brother the farm labourer. In India four men, and sturdy men too, are employed to draw the rickshaw of a lady. In Japan one man breaks his heart, up hill and down dale, dragging a full-grown European male.

Draught horses, draught donkeys, and draught dogs are especially legislated for in the countries wherein they are used; it yet remains for the poor draught biped of Japan to be relieved of half his burden. Many are finely developed, healthy young fellows; but very many are poor, sickly, weak-chested men, prematurely old, who are an exact prototype of the overworked, under-fed cab-horse of the London streets twenty years ago. Like many other foreigners, I was under the impression that the rickshaw was an indigenous vehicle, and had always looked upon it as one of the most typical remnants of Old Japan. Quite otherwise, it is a part of the new civilisation, and was invented, and introduced, by an American missionary. The inventor supplied the exact vehicle to suit the country, as is demonstrated by its universal adoption throughout the land; it remains for the Legislature to regulate the blessing in such a way as to prevent its use from becoming a cancer in the side of the future manhood of Japan.

Our first regular halt was at Mishima, a straggling village at the foot of the hills, where we found a very clean and comfortable little Japanese inn. Our toy, paper rooms, fifteen feet square and seven feet high, faced inwards from the road towards the diminutive Japanese garden. A Japanese garden is generally about ten yards square, and in this small space is found a complete park and demesne, with lake, summerhouses, temples, trees, all complete, and all in keeping with the dimensions available. The lake is four feet long and full of small gold-fish; on the border stands an old, old pine-tree exactly eighteen inches high, and *fifty years old*; beneath its shade is a Shinto temple carved out of one piece of stone the size of a brick; on a lofty crag, some two and a half feet high, stands a fine maple tree, perfect in form and shape, fifteen years old and twelve inches high; round the corner, in a sunny spot, is a prolific orange-tree eighteen inches high, with one full-sized ripe orange on it (the only disproportioned occupant of the garden). The production of these miniature trees is a fine art known only to the Japanese gardener. We bought three of them later : a maple, a pine, and a bamboo clump, each about fifteen years old and eighteen inches to two feet high, growing in shallow dishes. Abundant directions for their nurture were received, but whether they will still live in our hands remains to be seen. Carrying lilliputianism still further, we were told of a complete garden contained in a shallow two-dozen wine-case. Everything was complete, down to the fish in the lake, a sheet of water only a few inches square, and the foot-bridges over the watercuts. Tea-houses there were, and numerous trees of various kinds, each about six inches high : old as the hills these, but full of vitality and yet never growing bigger. Needless to say, a special gardener had to be kept up for this tiny gem, and his wages were those of an archbishop.

In a Japanese inn one sits on the floor, eats on the floor, sleeps on the floor. But the wind is tempered to the shorn lamb, for the floors are laid with deep soft mats, marvels of neatness and cleanliness. An ample lunch-basket (observe the old soldier), stocked with all the necessaries of life down to a bottle of curry-powder, sufficiently supplies the deficiencies of the Japanese *cuisine*, and we eat and sleep in much comfort. Then up and away again in the merry rickshaw, with death's-head in the shafts. Our next halting place, after a short run, was Numadzu, at another entirely Japanese inn. No one could be kinder and more hospitable than our hosts: the whole household was in a continuous bustle from first to last, doing its utmost to make us comfortable. Here was to be found that glorious institution, the common bath : this structure consisted of a large wooden box always full of water, at nearly boiling-point. It was placed exactly inside the main entrance to the inn, and by way of seclusion was surrounded by *glass* windows. The whole inn—men, women, children, and travellers—take a turn at this bath in the course of the evening. My own modest dash afforded much amusement to the maids, for, wishing to spare their blushes as much as possible, I made one bound from my last garment into the bath; but the next bound surpassed it in agility, carrying me out and beyond, for the water was hot enough to boil a lobster.

The beds they make up for one are most comfortable, even luxurious. Piles of wadded quilts are laid on the floor, then our own sheets and pillows, then a blanket for early morning use. A huge mosquito-net, nearly as large as the room, is then rigged up, being supported by cords from the four corners of the room. It is not a case of a bed with mosquito-nets, but a bed in the centre of a commodious mosquito-marquee. These nets are dark green, and the mesh is fine enough to keep out the smallest sand-fly. Contrary to every expectation, the weather in the plains was perfectly cool—68° at night, and not above 84° in the hottest part of the day. The people of the inn were immensely amused at the Japanese sentences I used to grind out to them, taken from a colloquial book; indeed, nothing sounds funnier than to hear any foreigner read out, say, 'Please bring me some tea,' like a sermon out of a book. Our bill, including two meals, beer, aerated waters, and rickshaw to the station, was $3. Economy and novelty combined.

A long day's railway work brought us to Lake Biwa—and a very disagreeable inn at the village of Hikoné. We here met young Japan—he of the smattering of English and the European hat—in the person of the proprietor. Rapacity, incivility, inhospitality, be for evermore written over the portals of the Raku-raku Inn. The truth of the matter is that the proprietor does not want foreign visitors, and therefore, I conclude, makes them systematically uncomfortable, and charges them exorbitantly. Imagine paying $5 for the use of a small room for one night, without food or even a bath, devoured by mosquitoes, fleas, and—the natural-enemy-of-man. The first query of our host was, 'When are you going?' and his natural boorishness only thawed to toleration when he heard that it would be 'at the very first possible moment.' We had intended making some stay here, for I was anxious to visit the famous battlefield on which the most renowned of the Shoguns defeated the rest of Japan, as well as the ancient castle and stronghold of the stern old daimio.

I forgot to mention the cormorant-fishing at Gifu. To us, who take a great interest in hawking, the subject was especially interesting. As with hawks, the motive is hunger; and each cormorant is fitted with a metal ring round his neck, which prevents his swallowing the larger fish. Six, eight, or even twelve cormorants are employed at one time, and directed by one man, each bird having a waist-band to which is attached a twelve-foot rein of spruce fibre. This bunch of twelve reins the master holds in his left hand. A lighted lantern—for it is night-time—attracts the fish to the neighbourhood of the boat, and then the cormorants are set to work diving and catching them. A good cormorant will catch from 100 to 150 good-sized fish in one hour, besides the smaller ones which he has swallowed to appease his own appetite.

The *Times* of July 17th, 1889, contains an admirable letter on the subject by Major-General Palmer, R.E.

As the steamer plying down the lake did not start till 10 A.M., an early rise enabled us to get a very fair idea of the castle and its defences. Speaking generally, it cannot be better described than by saying that it is a solidly constructed masonry-and-wood, three-storied blockhouse, perched on a hillock about 150 feet above lake-level. In irregular rings round it, each lower than the other, run three solid masonry walls, ten to twenty feet thick, ten to forty feet high, and very massive. The lower of these is on the level plain, and includes the wet ditch and all the stables and out-buildings. The whole interior of the defences is densely wooded with trees of probably 100 years' growth. As a modern defence, even with the trees cut down, the old stronghold would be worse than useless—merely a trap for catching the attackers' shells: but when we think of the days of bows and arrows and swords, the immense strength of the place is irresistibly manifest. The walls are some 300 years old, the local guide affirmed, and they are as good as new now. On neighbouring hills, within long cannon range, used to stand the eyries of other great daimios. We can well imagine the old gentlemen, bristling with knives, each seated on his own hill, watching from year's end to year's end for a chance of pouncing on a less ready neighbour, and exterminating him and his clan and castle for ever. The view from the castle is very fine, and takes in the greater part of Lake Biwa.

At 10 A.M. a funny little steamer came puffing and fussing and whistling alongside, and took us and our goods on board. The lake is some thirty-six miles long, and to us, coming from fairer scenes, appeared tame and uninteresting. Four hours' journey, mostly spent in sleep to repair the ravages of the previous night, brings our little vessel to Otsu, at the western corner of the lake. Till a couple of years ago no one had ever heard of Otsu, but it has now become famous as the scene of the so-called attempt on the life of the Czarewitch. How many English people must have exclaimed at the time: 'Thank goodness this did not take place in India!' Half the world, and certainly the whole of France, would have instantly discovered that the attempted assassination was the result of a deeply laid plot on the part of the British Government. Here is an extract, let us say, from the *République Française*, dated May 12th, 1891:—'With regret the most profound we find ourselves obliged to announce to the people of Paris and the French nation yet another instance of the barbarous and inhuman conduct of that perfidious Albion whose insolent demeanour is the reproach of Europe, and whose poisoned grasp is throttling the life out of our amiable ally, the Khedive of Egypt. Having enticed the Czarewitch, the son of their hereditary foe, to India, a hired assassin, paid with English gold, has accomplished the rest. Shall such a nation remain within the pale of the comity of civilised people? A thousand thunders—No! she is henceforth ejected, divorced.' Here follows a perfect Augean stableful of abuse, winding up with a ra-ta-ta-ta-bom-BOM. The French newspaper man, when he loses his head, becomes very amusing. The above is about on a par with the information afforded to the French public during the present Franco-Siamese difficulty, where, of course, the 'perfidious one' is at her perfidy again, and thwarting the aspiration of the chosen nation.

Otsu is a small, highly uninteresting place, used generally as a starting-point for tours on Lake Biwa. The Czarewitch, intent on some such tour, was passing along the street, when one of the policemen, specially detailed for his protection, drew his short sword of office and made an attack on the prince. Luckily, the two rickshaw men were active and courageous fellows, and immediately seized and disarmed the would-be assassin. He proved to be an old soldier, who had served with distinction against the rebels in the Satsuma campaign, and like many old soldiers had a grievance, and considered this an effective method of bringing it to notice. That he really meant to assassinate the Czarewitch is highly improbable. It is an ill wind that blows no one any good, and that day brought a fortune to the two rickshaw men. They received $5000 each for their services, which sum is, of course, to men of their degree an independence for life. One, we hear, bought a piece of land, and is living *en prince* on a small scale ; whilst the other worked unremittingly for the space of two years in the endeavour to swallow his pension in the form of saké, the wine of the country. Failing, however, we are informed by a daily paper that he has ' turned over a new leaf, and now has 200 hens:' a kind of chicken nunnery, apparently. History does not relate what became of the policeman; not improbably he and his petition were transferred to a realm where grievances are no more.[1] Characteristically enough the townspeople were so ashamed of the inhospitality of their townsfellow that they petitioned the Mikado to change the name of the town, whose fair fame was now for ever sullied.

[1] We afterwards heard he died in prison.

A semi-Japanese inn gave us shelter here —an inn which aspired to chairs, and tables, and chicken cutlets, but the bedrooms were small and stuffy. Perhaps the best way to see Lake Biwa is to work from Kyoto, making a day or two's excursion of it; but to us it seemed at best an uninteresting sheet of water.

One and a half hour's ride by rickshaw, or a pleasant morning's walk, and we reach Kyoto, the ancient capital of the empire, and for many hundred years the place which contained the gilded cage in which generations of Mikados were born, and lived, and died, unseen of their subjects, unknown to them, semi-deities whilst they lived, and yet nigh powerless for good or ill.

CHAPTER XIV

THE ANCIENT CAPITAL OF THE MIKADO

HERE at Kyoto we returned to civilisation and newspapers, and found that the world had been getting on very well without us. But again the same discordant note in the papers, and again Mr. Clement Scott and his somewhat acrid criticisms: this time transplanted from the *Illustrated London News*. It is hardly possible to agree with such wholesale condemnation—condemnation which savours somewhat of antagonism. Perhaps a feeling of disappointment dictated words which the mellowing hand of a few weeks will cause to seem harsh even to the writer. The Japanese public, with perhaps natural harshness, ascribe Mr. Scott's attitude to a not very temperate desire to disagree with writers to whom Japan and and all things Japanese would appear to be sacred. Poor Japan! let us come and go as friendly visitors, let us as far as in us lies neither gush over nor garrotte her.

The politeness of the Japanese is likened to that of the French—merely surface-deep. Whether this is true or not, there is certainly another trait in their character which closely resembles the French. They are quick to anger. If history is to be trusted, a spark, and the whole country is in a blaze. It is not intended to infer that unfriendly foreign criticism in itself is strong enough to light such a spark, but merely that it prepares the way. During our short stay, so unpopular were foreigners in some quarters that we saw it gravely and earnestly urged, in the Japanese daily press, that foreigners should again be forcibly ejected from the land. 'Japan for the Japanese' was the cry. If a spark like this were perchance to catch the quick-match of popular enthusiasm, one of the most appalling massacres of any age might be the very possible result.

Speaking of Japanese newspapers generally and the liberty of the press in particular, the author of *Things Japanese* gives the following interesting paragraph : 'Imprisonment for press offences is very common. In March 1890, an offending editor was condemned to captivity for no less a term than four years and a half. So openly has imprisonment come to be reckoned among the inevitable incidents of a journalistic career, that most papers employ what is called a "prison editor," that is, a man who, though nominally editor-in-chief, has little or nothing to do but to go to prison when the paper gets into trouble. . . . In fact, the traditional Japanese fondness for dual offices has cropped up again in modern guise. Formerly there was an Emperor *de jure* and an Emperor *de facto*. . . . Now there are real editors and dummy prison-editors.'

Eleven hundred years ago the reigning Mikado made Kyoto his capital, and built unto himself a palace. With one short interruption, that palace was occupied by his successors in the title till the revolution of 1868. There is nothing new under the sun: here is a city founded eleven hundred years ago, which is laid out with the mathematical precision, and rectangular exactness of the newest townlet, in the newest country. The town is a checkboard, all the streets running due north and south, or due east and west. Perhaps no greater contrast exists than the contrast between the former capital of the Mikado, the semi-spiritual, semi-temporal Emperor of Japan, and that of his first subject, but actual lord and master, the great military chief, the Shogun at Tokyo. Tokyo was, and is, for the old walls still stand like adamant, a huge fortified town; the fortress within a fortress, the citadel being the Shogun's own abode. Within the encircling walls each fierce and warlike daimio had his own little fortified enclosure, or castle, and was yearly compelled to occupy it for six months, as an act of submission to the Shogun. In a word, Tokyo might have been described as a large fortified camp, where stone enclosures took the place of tents—for the plans of some of these old Japanese towns curiously resembles the form of a modern canvas camp.

In Kyoto, on the contrary, we come across

the mild and placid features of an open defenceless town — the only stronghold near being the Saturday-to-Monday abode of the Shogun, when he made his yearly visit. A high garden wall was the mild Mikado's only defence. Where might is right, and, despite arbitration companies and peace societies, big battalions will in all probability rule the world to the end, it is not difficult to imagine how low the power of the Mikado must have sunk, before the daily growing evidence of the physical might of his vassal. As dissimilar as the Mikado was from the Shogun, so unlike were his followers to those of the military dictator. Here mild and peaceful nobles, with lineage of untold antiquity, but whose inclinations lay in the direction of the cloister rather than the clash of arms, took the place of the stalwart daimios, to whom war was as the breath of life. The latter appeared mere *parvenus*, hired cut-throats of the Shogun, to the ancient nobility. To the daimios, these placid relics of antiquity appeared beneath contempt; they classed them, as far as man-

CALCULATING MACHINE

hood went, with priests and women. Be well assured the astute Shogun fostered and fanned this notion.

But the whirligig of time has changed all that: the Shogun and his daimios are themselves mere relics of the past. The Mikado, quitting his calm seclusion, has donned a military uniform, and taken up his abode in the Shogun's stronghold at Tokyo. Kyoto as a capital is deserted, it has shrunk to half its size, and is now chiefly noticeable for the excellency of its silk and cloisonné shops.

Look at this staid merchant with his calculating-board; he is typical of the Kyoto of to-day, a quiet business town. The abacus or calculating-board is an indispensable adjunct to every tradesman's stock throughout China and Japan. To us it looks cumbrous, but those who have been born to it do their sums of addition and subtraction with wonderful celerity on it. I took lessons in its use. Its principle is thus tersely explained by Professor Chamberlain: Each of the five beads in the broad lower division of the board represents one unit, and each solitary bead in the narrow upper division represents five units. Each vertical column is thus worth ten units. Furthermore, each vertical column represents units ten times greater than those in the column immediately to the right of it, exactly as in our system of notation by means of Arabic numerals. Any sum in arithmetic can be done on the abacus, even to the extracting of square and cube roots.

Without doubt this is the spot where the traveller can most efficiently, and with the greatest satisfaction to himself, exchange dollars for the produce of the country. Any hotel manager will direct him to the best shops, and he will find there English spoken,— Japanned English, perhaps, but quite enough for all purposes. The term 'Japanned English' reminds me of Professor Chamberlain's very entertaining article on that subject in his book, *Things Japanese*. The police force are enjoined to learn English, and a few useful short conversations are given in the pamphlet under review by the Professor.

'Here is one between a representative of the force and an English blue-jacket :—

'*Q.* What countryman are you?

'*A.* I am a sailor belonging to the *Golden Eagle*, the English man-of-war.

'*Q.* Why do you strike this Jinrikisha man?

'*A.* He told me impolitely.

'*Q.* What does he told you impolitely?

'*A.* He insulted me, saying loudly, "The sailor! the sailor!" when I am passing here.

'*Q.* Do you strike this man for that?

'*A.* Yes.

'*Q.* But do not strike him, for it is forbided.

'*A.* I strike him no more.

'Exit blue-jacket much edified.

'The author teaches his policeman not only to converse but to moralise. Thus :—

'Japanese police force consists of nice young men. But I regret their attires are not perfectly neat. When a constable come in conduct with a people he shall be polite and tender in his manner of speaking and movement.

'If he will terrify or scold the people with enormous voice, he will become himself an object of fear for the people.

'Civilised people is meek, but barbarous people is vain and haughty.

'A cloud-like writing of Chinese character and

performance of the Chinese poem, or cross hung on the breast, would no more worthy to pretend others to avail himself to be a great man.

'Those Japanese who acquired a little of foreign anguage think that they have the knowledge of foreign countries, as Chinese, English, or French. There is nothing hard to success what they attempt.

'They would imitate themselves to Caesar, the ablest hero of Rome, who has been raised the army against his own country crossing the Rabicon.

'A gleam of diffidence seems to cross the police mind when one policeman says to the other, "You speak the English very well," and the other replies, "You jest."'[1]

They say that every one who comes to Japan sooner or later falls a victim to the mania for buying all sorts and conditions of things, useful or useless, ornamental or the reverse, it matters not, but buy they must. Kyoto is perhaps as good a place as any for giving rein to this amiable weakness, but the more prudent will fix beforehand the size of the cheque to be spent, and flee the city the moment it is expended. Other-

[1] *Things Japanese,* by Professor Basil Hall Chamberlain.

wise financial chaos for the rest of the tour. We, I think, fell most hopelessly in the old brocade line. It began with a sneaking admiration for an ancient daimio's costume, and ended in the course of a week in our buying out the shop. Now that the fever is off, and the last cent has departed, not the least sense of shame or regret comes over us. We should probably do the same again next week. The old costumes are wonderfully handsome and picturesque, and everything, down to elaborate wigs, swords, fans, and tobacco-pouch, is complete. Next a 'sword' era set in, and we are now in possession of sufficient swords to arm a small squadron. Then we got on to cloissonne and satsuma ware; and here it may be remarked in parentheses that a very large cheque goes a very short way where the best of these wares are concerned. A little coolness now set in, and we descended to cheap and effective things in the doll, fan, and umbrella line. A slight rise again in porcelain, books, and pictures; followed by a decline towards cotton dressing-gowns and photographs, and then a rapid but dignified withdrawal to Osaka.

Every one's object probably is to get things that are not seen in England, and if possible for less than they cost in London. We were fairly successful; quite as much so as was to be expected. The prices in the larger shops are fixed, and no percentage is allowed for ready money. Other dealers, on the contrary, ask more than they expect, and are quite open to an offer. Perhaps it is hardly necessary to mention that, as in India, China, and all Eastern countries, much patience and complete command of temper are *sinê qua non* in any bargain. Bargaining is the salt of life to most Eastern dealers, and there are many who would, I believe, rather lose a little at the end of a courteous interval of bargaining, than gain that amount by an instant sale to an irascible Western.

Like all Japanese towns, Kyoto is best seen at night. The scene is then fairyland indeed, with its thousands of brightly coloured lanterns. On the river these appear to special advantage, for the water being shallow, clusters of permanent platforms stud the stream, and these at night are turned into tea-houses brightly lighted up. Along the shore from each house abuts a similar structure, so that all the world and its wife sit nightly down by the cool water's edge. On some of the small shingle islands are not only tea-houses, but the small booths of a country fair.

Tanks too are sunk and stocked with small fish, and for a few coppers rod and line are supplied, and the ingenuous youth angles for sprats. A stout lady presides over an emporium of buns, each bun to be won by a well-directed shot at a figure with a puff-and-dart. An immense capacity for enjoyment in a small way pervades the whole scene.

We visited again a theatre, but it was of a poor class compared to that of Tokyo. The etceteras, however, gave us ample food for amusement. When we arrived the curtain was down, and an extended game of hide-and-seek was being performed by all the children of the audience, in and out of the drop scene and side wings. After some delay a mild-looking person in the corner beat two pieces of bamboo together; this was the call-bell: up went the curtain, and off scuttled all the little boys and girls to their places. The play is not worth describing in detail, but there were one or two instructive novelties in stage management. For instance, in the opening scene, where two magnificent people were talking to each other, an ordinary everyday person was walking up and down behind them reading a book. We thought at first he was part of the play, but found out later that he was the prompter! And not only prompter, but also stage manager and general director of all things—even unbending so far at one portion of the play as to walk to the front of the stage, and quietly but firmly removing a small boy who insisted on sitting on the edge.

The supers, who at Tokyo wore black masks and dresses, here wore no disguise, and just strolled about the stage as the spirit moved them. To us foreigners the arrival of the actors by a raised platform through the middle of the audience is quaint enough, but it is quainter still when the chief daimio, making a state entry, in great magnificence, happens to be followed, at 2 ft. interval, by the programme-man. We treated the rickshaw man to a seat, for which small mercy he never ceased to be grateful. These people appreciate little presents and little indulgences far more than the stereotyped 'tip.'

One is constrained to wonder when these people of Kyoto sleep. Coming home from the theatre late at night, all the shops are open, and blazing with lanterns. In the earliest morning there they are, open as usual. All night long we hear pedlars going round, as if it were mid-day; and as each pedlar either rings a bell or beats a drum we naturally wish them at the bottom of the sea. It may be said, literally, that there is not a moment's quiet, from dusk to dawn, in the midst of a town like this.

Like our old ruffian, the *chowkidar* of India, the watchmen here are employed more to scare away thieves than to catch them. In India the *chowkidar* arms himself with a small assortment of bloodthirsty-looking weapons and mounts guard over your house. But he has not the remotest intention of wading about in any one's gore—certainly not in his own. When he makes his rounds therefore he takes care to let every one know that he is on the move by loud coughs and clearings of the throat. The thief takes the hint and avoids a rencontre which is sought for by neither party. In Japan the watchman acts on the same principle, but instead of clearing his throat he beats two pieces of bamboo together. Consequently he and the thief rarely meet.

A special permit is required to see the interior of the Mikado's old palace, and that of the Shogun, now also called an Imperial palace, but the outside sufficiently impresses one with the humbleness of the former and the military strength of the latter. From the descriptions of the interiors they must be very poor; indeed, one writer goes so far as to say that during his visit not even a sheet of note-paper could the palace produce, so sordid was the poverty of its lord. At the back of this modest abode, where the descendant of eleven centuries of Emperors till lately lived, rises a sufficiently magnificent mansion, with a fine turret and range of buildings in the European style; tastefully designed, and well and substantially built of brick, faced with massive grey granite. A modern palace for the Emperor, no doubt? Indeed no; this is the humble resting-place of the American missionaries. The more one sees of it, the more fascinated one becomes with this magnificent career. A British subaltern becomes food for powder at the exceedingly limited figure of 5s. 6d. per diem : he is evidently wasting his opportunities.

At the back of the Chion-in temple we found an ancient house, the residence of the Shogun Iemitsu about 250 years ago, and still used occasionally by the Mikado's son and heir. The screens in this house are beautifully painted, and considering their age and the constant use a screen undergoes, in excellent preservation. Our rickshawman whispered a few scandalous remarks regarding the use made of the apartments by the High Priest, which if they are common property will hardly add much to the credit of the Shinto religion.

There are one or two gardens in the vicinity, which are mentioned by some books as worthy of a visit; perhaps so, if one has nothing better to do, but they are poor in the extreme, small, untidy, and to our eyes inartistic. On the way to one of these is passed a very fine piece of engineering. The level of Lake Biwa is some 300 ft. above Kyoto, and a range of hills several hundred feet high intervenes between them. It occurred to a young student at the Engineering College, Tokyo, that not only could an irrigation canal be constructed to tap the lake for the benefit of the crops below, but also that a navigable outlet and inlet for boats was a feasible project. His plans were submitted to the Government, and were approved of; and he, a mere schoolboy, was there and then intrusted with the task of executing his project. Tunnelling through the hills, the two canals separate at Keage, and go swishing down the contours of the hills at the rate of 10 ft. a second—too rapid, of course, for any boat to make way against. But the obstacle, if not faced, is at any rate turned by an inclined cable-tram. The boats are placed bodily, cargo and all, on to these cars, and run up the line to the higher level, or *vice versa*. The undertaking cost only one and a half million dollars, and the boy-engineer's fame and fortune were made.

Though it was now the end of July we found Kyoto much cooler than we expected, 82° to 84° as a rule, though a degree or two higher on occasion. The hottest part of the day in Japan is undoubtedly the afternoon. We were almost invariably out as late as noon, shopping or sight-seeing, without feeling the heat, yet as late in the afternoon as five o'clock the temperature was often unpleasantly high, and the heat more oppressive than at midday.

CHAPTER XV

OSAKA TO THE END

A SHORT journey of ninety minutes by train from Kyoto brings one to Osaka, celebrated for its castle, the number of troops stationed there, and the water scene at night. Our visit was a purely professional one, connected with the troops, and the climate was far too sultry to allow of our taking any but a jaundiced view of the place. 91° Fahrenheit at 8 P.M., without punkahs, or other visible means of support, reminds one of the most turgid nights in June in Upper India. Moreover, there are probably more mosquitoes and sand-flies in Osaka than in the rest of the Japanese Empire put together. Professionally our visit was eminently a success; socially, except from the point of view of the mosquito and his little friend, it was a failure. In the next edition of Dante's *Inferno*, let me recommend the following torture as worthy to have a place alongside the serpents and the lake of sulphurous flames. A small and thoroughly stuffy room into which not a breath of air penetrates; the thermometer at 120°; a very soft and fiery hot pillow for the victim's head, who should of course be very tired and sleepy. Introduce 1000 mosquitoes who have been starved for a week, and 2500 sand-flies who have not tasted flesh for a fortnight. Stir well up and leave till the morning. Outside, steam whistles, pedlars' bells, and 'we-won't-go-home-till-morning' songs to be supplied at intervals. I have never tried sleeping with serpents or in sulphurous flames; but if they are worse than a bedroom in Osaka in August, heaven help the serpents!

But there is one great and redeeming feature even in August, and that is the river after dark. To be appreciated, it must be seen; descriptions fail miserably before the cool comfort of drifting along between brightly lighted shores, through a throng of boats all gaily decorated with lanterns. Little boys tumble overboard and swim about like young ducks, and little girls tinkle, tinkle on their guitars like—like anything. Big boys and big girls laugh and chat, and no doubt flirt, together; and old men and old maidens look on, and smile, and encourage the soft dalliance. In and out, up and down, round and round, ply vendors of all sorts: fruit, lemonade, and cakes, beer and ice, macaroni and supper dishes; last, but not least, the firework-pedlars. All do a brisk trade, and especially these last; fireworks are part of the scene, and part of the every evening life of the citizen of Osaka. Not puny crackers or juvenile squibs, but really first-class rockets, and catherine-wheels, and snakes of fire on the water. How late this midnight water-picnic is kept up we had no means of accurately ascertaining: from dusk to dawn, most probably, for the first query on engaging a boat was, 'Do you want it all night?' Those who visit Osaka in the heat, and are not afraid of fever, cannot do better than take a boat for the night and sleep on the cool tideway.

From Osaka, the fine old park and temples of Nara can be reached in an hour and a half by train. Here red fallow-deer attack you for biscuits, and the sacred pony fumes and fusses and squeals and stamps until you give him a handful of beans. A group of dancing-girls perform the sacred dance for hire, and innocent villagers attempt to sell to the guileless foreigner appalling wooden atrocities, sad libels on the graceful fallow-deer. In one part of the park stands the temple, which contains the Daibutsu, an enormous bronze figure, which, seated, measures fifty-three feet in height. Behind the image, amidst a collection of relics, we came across the mummy of an undoubted mermaid. It was in very good preservation, and showed distinctly a human head, with the body and tail of a fish. The head was as large as that of a small boy, and the body was that of a good-sized salmon, some thirty to thirty-six inches long. This curiosity is not mentioned by any writers, so far as my researches go.

O Yasumi, that Honourable Repose of

which this book is the record, was now drawing to a close; a few days more, and the familiar engine would be again throbbing, and our long sea-voyage back to work in the 'land of regrets' would begin. Those days we elected to spend at the waters of Takaradzuka (but what is in a name?), in the green country on the banks of an enticing trout-stream. Here, amidst the simple countryfolks, we passed our last days in Japan, and left with the kindly farewell in our ears, 'Sayona,[1] please come again.' I think we shall.

[1] Farewell.

CHAPTER XVI

FINANCIAL AND GENERAL

THE subject of travelling expenses is one which everybody avoids as much as possible. I have avoided it as long as is decent, but it has to be faced at last. In dealing with the expenses in a country like Japan, of course we will confine ourselves entirely to the ordinary items of hotel bills, railway fares, and travelling about generally. To enter into the regions of curio-buying is to enter into a vast and incomprehensible world of conjecture. No man himself knows to what depths of extravagance he will sink in this land of things to be bought; and it would certainly be out of the question for a third person to venture to define any limit one way or the other to this expenditure. One suggestion, however, we will make, and that is, to fix beforehand the amount that is available for expenditure, irrespective of travelling expenses, and, if possible, to stick to that amount.

The cost of reaching Japan naturally varies with the distance of the starting-point. From London to Yokohama and back, *viâ* the Suez Canal and Hong Kong, will cost £115 first-class and £65 second-class, travelling by P. and O. The other way round—that is, from London to Yokohama, *viâ* Canada or America—will cost about £80 first-class and £55 second-class. From London to London, making a complete circuit of the world, and calling in at Japan and other places, costs only £125 first-class.

From India the cheapest and most direct route is from Calcutta, *viâ* Singapore and Hong Kong. A *return* ticket to Yokohama is priced at Rs.580,[1] one of the opium-boats of Messrs. Jardine or Messrs. Apcar taking the traveller as far as Hong Kong, and the P. and O., Messageries Maritimes, or Canadian Pacific lines carrying one on.

The hotels of India are atrocious—it is a

[1] Equal to about £39 at 1s. 4d. to the rupee.

standing byword; but at the same time they are very cheap. There is not an hotel in the land in which board and lodging cannot be obtained for Rs.7, or 9s. 4d., *per diem*. This includes breakfast, lunch, dinner, early morning tea-and-toast and afternoon tea-and-toast, hot water, lighting, attendance—in fact, everything.

At Singapore we come to the region of dollars and a slight improvement in accommodation at about Indian prices. Chinese servants supplant the atrocities of an Indian hotel, and we take a step up in the empire of cleanliness.

It is not till we reach Hong Kong that we come across anything approaching Western civilisation in the matter of hotels. Here we find the immense structures and civilised comforts of large hotels in Europe. Electric lights and bells, lifts, carpets, good furniture, good attendance, and a good table. Naturally, however, the prices charged are higher. We pay here $5 a day for a good room, as against $3 at Singapore, or Rs.6 or Rs.7 in India. The additional comfort is well worth the difference in price. Would that the public and the hotel proprietors in India would grasp this notion!

In Japan we find, as in any European country, every grade and class of hotel and inn, from the fine foreign structures of Yokohama and Tokyo to the clean and neat little inn indigenous to the country. The Grand Hotel at Yokohama and the Imperial Hotel at Tokyo would do credit to any town in England, and prices are about the same as at Hong Kong. The dearest hotel we visited was the Oriental Hotel, Kobé, and the charge there was $5 a day for a good room. Speaking generally, the cost *per diem* in the large hotels in the large towns need not be more than $3.50 for a bachelor, or $7 for a married couple. On the other hand, good accommodation cannot be found under $3 *per diem* for a bachelor, or $6 for a married couple.

In the hill resorts a considerable variety in prices will be found. At Nikko, at the Arai Hotel—a very small semi-Japanese hotel, but perhaps the most comfortable we visited in Japan—the charge was only $5 a day for a married couple, and $2.50 for a bachelor. At Ikao, at a similar hotel, though much inferior in comfort, we paid only $4.50 a day for two people. The Fujuja Hotel at Mujanoshita is more pretentious, and larger, than these latter, and there the charge again rises to $3.50 a-head *per diem*. On Hakoné Lake are a couple of Japanese inns where foreign food is supplied; the charge at these is $5 a day for a married couple, and $2.50 for a single person.

In the purely Japanese inns, where no foreign comforts in the shape of chairs and tables are provided, or anything but Japanese food supplied, we were generally charged from $1 to $1.50 a-head. A Japanese traveller would get identically the same accommodation for 50 cents. Here we have a great grievance against some of the authorities on Japan. With the best possible intentions, and as a hint for the private guidance of foreign travellers, it is laid down that we Europeans must expect to pay more for our accommodation than the

Japanese traveller, because we give more trouble to the management and require more attendance. Quite so; the principle is excellent, and not one of us would for a moment grudge a handsome 'tip' in recompense for the extra service received. But, unhappily, in these days of erudition the very people these instructions were *not* issued for, the hotel proprietors, have got hold of them, and deliberately charge double, treble, and even five times as much as they would a Japanese traveller, and in justification of the charge calmly point out the passage in the guide-book. In fact, we all resent being mulcted, as a right, of a sum of money which is really a gratuity. Imagine our feelings, for instance, at being asked $5 for a room, without food, for which a Japanese would pay 90 cents, and having our own guide-book hurled at our head, as a voucher, so to speak. Yet this happened to us at Hikoné (not to be confused with Hakoné).

Amongst Japanese hotel proprietors there is a sort of middle-class man, and that man is the abomination of desolation. He comes between the highly civilised proprietor, who keeps a first-class hotel, and whose charges are fixed and posted, and the aboriginal landlord of the country, who rarely sees a foreigner, and charges him as he would any other traveller. Our middle-man, on the other hand, has got a smattering of English (or his son has for him); and, like other semi-civilised beings, he has caught on to the evil characteristics of the foreigner first—in his case taking the form of rapacity and dishonest dealing.

In the matter of 'tips,' it is somewhat difficult to lay down exact rules. At some hotels the same 'boy' or woman—for some hotels have male attendants, some female, and some both—waits on one at meals, and also does the whole of one's bedroom work. Here the problem is much simplified, and a single person will find that a present calculated at the rate of twenty cents a day will well satisfy this attendant. Married couples will give perhaps half as much again. This refers to short sojourns of a week or under.

At hotels where one attendant waits at meals, whilst another does the bedroom work, the same total sum is sufficient—one-third going to the table servant and two-thirds to the bedroom attendant. In addition, a small fee, say twenty cents or so, should be given to the man who carries up one's luggage and often assists with the bath, cleaning boots, etc. With women servants a little present in kind is often more appreciated than a money present.

Intending visitors to Japan are often uncertain whether to engage a guide or not. Our advice is not to do so on any account. A guide, unless he is absolutely indispensable, is always a nuisance in any country—and a very expensive nuisance, too. In Japan, a guide will very nearly double one's expenses ; in fact, Jones might give his friend Smith a free trip through Japan for very little more than the free trip he provides his guide with. A guide's fee is a dollar a day; his hotel bills and railway fares have to be paid ; he of course requires a rickshaw to himself, travelling by road or merely sight-seeing a town, and another, or at any rate part of one, for his luggage. He knows nothing that cannot be found in Murray, his English is often elementary, and he becomes in a few days loathsome in one's eyes, as a sort of permanent task-master who relentlessly drags one here, there, and everywhere, whether one wants to or no. Moreover, every single article bought with the assistance of a guide costs about twenty-five per cent. more than if the purchase were made direct. Instead of helping his master, in nine cases out of ten the guide sides with his countryman in the making of any bargain. To those, of course, to whom money is no object the guide will no doubt save a great deal of trouble in arranging routes, engaging rickshaws, settling hotel bills, and other troublesome details. But he is a luxury.

No trouble will be experienced, either landing or embarking, with the custom-house officials, if one is perfectly civil and perfectly patient. On landing we were not delayed five minutes, and on embarking not two minutes, though we had nine cases of purchases. The slightest incivility or impatience may cause one infinite delay and trouble, as some of our fellows found to their cost.

No foreigner may travel inland beyond what is called the twenty-four-mile radius of the treaty ports without a passport. These passports are obtained through the traveller's national consul at the port of landing. A charge of a dollar is made for it.

There are posts, telegraphs, and railways all over the country, so the traveller may set his mind at rest on those points.

As in every other part of the globe, the most satisfactory coin to possess is the English sovereign, or letters of credit or circular notes representing sovereigns. Any bank will cash these into the coin of the country. The silver dollar, called in Japan a *yen*, is the standard coin of the country; and as the dollar fluctuates, so does the *yen*. But the actual circulating medium is paper money, the most general being for sums of ten, five, and one *yen*. The decimal parts of a *yen* are circulated in small silver and nickel coins. Most convenient for the traveller, this paper money: a silver dollar is an impossible coin to carry about in one's pocket, and fifty of them no pocket on earth will stand. Would that we had a paper rupee in India, to the everlasting benefit of our clothes! A dollar is at this date (August '93) worth exactly half-a-crown; therefore, a sovereign buys eight of them—which is good for the sovereign: it is not so long ago that a sovereign was worth only five dollars. At the same date (August '93) two rupees equal one dollar; but silver is unstable, and therefore the intending traveller must be prepared for fluctuations in value.

Taken all round, the autumn is the best time to visit Japan. The spring is often very wet, the summer too hot, and the winter too cold. The thermometer registered 94° in our rooms at Kobé in August. In the winter it freezes hard, and snow lies many inches deep over the greater part of Japan; and no one likes rain. The autumn, on the other hand, is bright, clear, and the climate delightful. The seasons are not rigidly defined, as in India, for instance; but they are somewhat more regular than in England.

The language is an exceedingly easy one to get a smattering of—sufficient, indeed, for travelling purposes—but a difficult one to master. An hour a day at words and sentences out of Murray's *Guide* will very soon supply one's linguistic requirements. Very handy little vocabularies are also to be purchased.

A general retrospect leads one to reiterate Charles Dickens's advice against entering a new country with preconceived opinions about it. In Japan this is especially advisable. Old residents call it the 'land of disillusions.' We need not go so far as that if we avoid loading ourselves with illusions before we land. Some writers have 'gushed' egregiously, no doubt; and the traveller who has only read such works runs a fair chance of being disappointed. Japan is a most interesting and beautiful spot; but let us avoid falling into the error of expecting to see scenery, and spectacles, and architecture, unequalled in other parts of the world. Country scenes in parts of England are as beautiful as any in Japan; there are no lakes to equal in beauty those of Lucerne, Como, and Maggiore; the Inland Sea is outrivalled by the scenery amongst the Philippine Islands; no town or harbour in Japan can for a moment compare in beauty or commodious safety with Hong Kong; the climate, though better than that of England, cannot claim the excellence of that of New Zealand; and so on, in a hundred matters. Let us go to this new country unbiassed for good or evil, and we shall probably enjoy our visit immensely, and come away with a happy recollection of it. Let us go there expecting to deal in nothing but superlatives, and we shall be egregiously disappointed.

CHAPTER XVII

THE ARMY OF JAPAN

THROUGH the courtesy of Mr. de Bunsen, British *chargé-d'affaires*, I received an introduction to the War Minister, Count Oyama, who very kindly gave me every facility for examining the Japanese army at leisure, both in and out of barracks.

It has been my privilege recently to study in some detail and on the spot the armies of France, Germany, Italy, and Belgium, besides those of Great Britain and India; and I will hasten to acknowledge that I was more than astonished at the military efficiency of the Japanese army, and more especially of the infantry portion of it. Let me confess that I was prepared to find a grotesque imitation of European armies, such as may be found at Bangkok, or such as fought under Arabi Pacha's standard at Tel-el-Kebir; but on the contrary I had the gratification of meeting troops who would do credit to any army in Europe. This being my opinion, I make bold to criticise it in the same serious manner as would be employed in dealing with the army of a Western nation.

When feudalism received its death-blow in 1868, and the undisciplined bands of armed followers of the martial daimios were disbanded, it became necessary, as at a corresponding epoch in European history, for a standing army to be raised for the defence of the throne and empire. With that happy directness which has characterised the best features of Japanese *renaissance*, she went straight to the best exponents of the military art in Europe, and intrusted implicitly the construction of her army to their hands. For her navy she went to Great Britain, the Queen of the Seas; for her army she went to France, then, as perhaps again now, the first military Power in Europe. A few years later the renown of the German victories led her to seek a change of instructors, and to German officers is due the credit of having completed the task so ably commenced by their French—shall we call them *confrères*? The Japanese army of to-day is therefore, as far as uniform and some minor points of instruction go, partly French and partly German. In the Emperor's bodyguard the uniform of the French Lancers is conspicuous, and he himself wears the scarlet kepi and trousers of a French officer; whilst at his gate stands sentry a soldier who might be on guard at the entrance of Strasburg or Metz.

Following the European model, the system of universal conscription has been introduced, and the army numbers 228,848 men of all arms. Of these, 113,229 belong to the reserve, and 53,137 to the territorial army. In the total are also included 1263 gendarmes, 1559 for the military colony in Yezo, and 3071 for the military schools. The peace strength, therefore, is 56,589,[1] and this is the number that may be calculated upon as available for ex-territorial campaigns.

[1] These figures are approximately accurate.

Formerly, as is still to some extent the case in India, there was a fighting class, called the *samurai*; and *samurai* and gentlemen became synonymous terms. No man was a gentleman unless he bore arms, and no man could remain a *samurai* and at the same time engage in trade—the two were incompatible. Now *samurai* and farmers and shopkeepers rub shoulders in the ranks of the same company of the same regiment. The conscription, as in Europe, catches all, be they highborn or menials, in the same huge net. Service with the colours is for three years, then nine years in the reserve, and then a last resting-place in the territorial army till the day of final absolution from military service.

As in our army, it was somewhat difficult to arrive at the exact pay drawn by a private soldier. An officer put the figure at about 10 cents per diem clear; a young *samurai*, who perhaps knew better, said that they got about ' 30 cents to spend on Sunday and all found by the State.' During the period of our visit the men were in summer uniform of white cotton drill. All arms and all branches of the service, with one or two exceptions, appear to be dressed alike, as in the German army: the band round the forage-cap being the only distinguishing feature. Thus, the Guards wear red bands; the Rifles black; the Line, Cavalry, Infantry, and Artillery yellow. No helmets are worn, all ranks being furnished with high, peaked forage-caps, as worn by German officers. In summer these have a white cover which leaves only the coloured band and peak visible. The Imperial Guard consists of some 6000 of all ranks, and is naturally the smartest and finest corps in the army.

The physique of the men is good, and may best be compared to that of the Goorkas of the Indian army. Small in stature, strongly built, sturdy, active, and with good marching legs, the Japanese soldier makes a stout little warrior. Of their fighting qualities it is impossible yet to speak with absolute confidence; but it must be remembered that for generations

Japan has possessed that martial spirit which compels success in war, and her sons have in all times, to no mean extent, been imbued with the first attribute of a soldier, personal courage. The only occasion on which the troops have had an opportunity of showing their mettle was during the Satsuma rebellion; and I am assured by an Englishman who was present at most of the engagements that their courage was beyond criticism.

The barrack accommodation is very good —in fact, much better than falls to the lot of British troops at Shorncliffe, or till lately at Aldershot. The buildings are mostly large, double-storied structures of wood, with numerous large windows, and thoroughly well ventilated. At Tokyo palatial brick barracks are in course of construction, and in time it is hoped to substitute brick for wood at all the other military centres. The men sleep in cots much as our soldiers do, and are supplied with good blankets and bedding.

The rations appeared good, ample, and

appetising; on one occasion I was present at the distribution of the dinners. Each man had his meal neatly laid out on a separate dish, and all these dishes lay, as many as a hundred together, in huge trays previous to distribution. On each plate was a good-sized fish and several little piles of vegetables and condiments, whilst rice, in large baskets and buckets, was distributed *ad lib*. The men looked stout and well nourished, doing good credit to their fare. Tea, which may be called the national beverage, is liberally supplied. That ultra-smartness and cleanliness which distinguishes a good British regiment is not to be found; but the troops are as smart and clean as those to be met with in any ordinary garrison town on the Continent —as much so, in fact, as is compatible with a short-service, conscript army.

In dealing with the army in detail, let us commence with the officers. Count Oyama's kind introduction brought a staff officer to our hotel at Osaka; and here, under his never-flagging guidance, with the thermometer at heaven knows what degree, I was enabled to see a good deal of the social and professional life of a Japanese officer. We first called on the general, who occupies a roomy mansion in the keep of the famous old castle—a castle which in all its walls and battlements is built of solid granite, now some 300 years old, but as strong and compact as on the day it was built. It lays no claim to be a modern stronghold, for it is too high and conspicuous to stand a bombardment by modern siege-guns—a fact tacitly acknowledged by the authorities, for no guns are mounted on its ramparts. An old bronze gun, of Chinese shape, displaying the Tokugawa crest, and used for saluting purposes, is the sole piece of ordnance visible.

Our next move was to the artillery lines, where we met the colonel commanding, who took us to the officers' mess. Many of the officers knew enough French for conversational purposes; but, curiously enough, we did not meet a single officer who spoke German, and, naturally, none who spoke English. This may perhaps be attributed to the fact that French was the original language of instruction, and the German officers, to avoid confusion, continued the training in the same language. In the navy, English is the foreign language which is most generally known. The mess is a large wooden building, with a good-sized dining-room and an ante-room, standing in a neat garden. Pictures and photographs hang on the wall; and a fine English map of the world and another of Japan cover the end of the room. In a corner are shelves on which are ranged specimens of modern projectiles, fuses, and other artillery samples. A blackboard, used for lecturing purposes, stands alongside. The officer who does most of the conversation calls the building 'le club des officiers.' The colonel calls it the 'canteen.' We should call it the 'officers' mess.' Whilst we are talking, coffee is handed round, made in (to me) a novel way. First sugar, and plenty of it, is placed in the cup, then hot water, and finally, at the moment of serving, a ball of ground coffee.

An infantry mess is built on much the

same lines, but is a good deal larger. There were sixty-four dining members in the one we visited. Here we met, in the officer commanding, a most jovial and cordial gentleman. Nothing short of beer at noonday was commensurate with his idea of hospitality; and, besides offering in the kindest manner information on every subject, he was eager to learn all he could about our troops, and especially those of the Indian army.

A Japanese subaltern officer receives from 29 to 32 dollars a month pay; a captain from 54 to 62 dollars; and the higher ranks in proportion—a colonel's pay being about 200 dollars. Officers pay for their messing, all taking their meals together. Chargers for mounted officers are supplied and kept by Government. The rates of promotion are much the same as in the Indian army—that is, 12 years to the rank of captain, 20 years to the rank of commandant (major), 26 years to a lieutenant-colonelcy, and 32 years to a full colonelcy.

In the cavalry mess we found the midday

meal was about to be served for twenty officers. The table was curiously characteristic of the country, where all else spoke more of Germany than of Japan. No cloth was laid, and opposite each officer on the polished board were placed one fan, one pair of chopsticks, one small bowl for saké,[1] and a box of patent safety-matches. Through the door appeared, borne by two men, a large tray on which twenty separate little dishes contained each officer's dinner. On the walls, besides regimental notices and rosters, hung a case of various-patterned horse-shoes, and a coloured engraving of a trooper of the British 5th Dragoon Guards.

Taken as a whole, the officers may be described as keen and energetic soldiers, having a thorough interest in, and taking great pains to perfect themselves in, the *minutiæ* of their profession. Perhaps as a personal item it may be permissible to add that their kindness and courtesy to a stranger will ever be gratefully remembered.

---

[1] Japanese wine, described by Professor Chamberlain as tasting like very weak sherry which has been kept in a beer-bottle.

The infantry of the army consists of six divisions of two brigades each. Each brigade is composed of two regiments, and each regiment has three battalions. The peace strength of a battalion is 400, its war strength 800. The rifle in use is a Japanese invention, and is named after its inventor, Muratta. It appears to be a modification of the Le Gros rifle—a breechloader, of course, with a simple and robust-looking breech action. There is no magazine attached. The rifle is sighted up to 1400 mètres, and the bore is about that of a Martini-Henry. The bayonet is of the 'sword-bayonet' pattern, well and securely fixed. A spring retains it in its scabbard when unfixed. These rifles are manufactured in Japan, but the barrels, I believe, come from England.

The drill of the infantry appeared exactly like that of the Germans. We had an opportunity of watching three battalions drilling together through a long morning. There was the same swing of the arm, the familiar 'parade march,' the well-known simple parade movements, that may be seen on a German garrison parade-ground : yet, curiously enough, the officer with us insisted that the drill was on the French model. As a matter of fact, all modern infantry drill is in its main elements remarkably similar. We may call it German, French, or English, but doubtless the origin is German. At the conclusion a well-executed attack was made, across an undulating piece of open ground, followed by a charge in line. The drill appeared to me remarkably good—certainly good enough for all practical purposes. Probably a very acute sergeant-major would have found faults here and there ; but, if so, they would have been in mere details, which by no means detracted from the efficiency of the regiment.

In barracks we came across a large party of men going through their daily bout with the bayonet. They had masks and fencing armour on, and, being told off in pairs, were hotly engaged. I was much impressed with their activity and address : certainly it would be difficult to take haphazard in our regiments so many men who seemed so thoroughly at home with this most difficult weapon. Perhaps an exaggerated respect for the breechloader has caused the subject of personal combat to sink into the background with us; whereas the traditions of hand-to-hand encounters are still fresh in the Japanese mind.

Let us next look at the cavalry. In opening this subject it will be remembered that I laid special stress on the excellence of the infantry. By that it was not intended to cast any slur on the other branches; it merely opened the door for an explanation of certain organic causes which enable a Japanese to become a better foot-soldier than cavalryman. Since the beginning of time the Japanese warrior has fought on foot, the two-handed sword and dagger being his chief weapons. In all the history of the past we have not yet been able to find an allusion to cavalry, and the only mounted man in a battle-scene is usually the chief.

Of course, there was a reason for this, for in a conflict before fire-arms were invented cavalry would have been invaluable. The first drawback to the employment of cavalry was the nature of the country. From end to end of it the empire is a huge, swampy rice-field; and where there are no rice-fields, there are mountains and forests. Next the scarcity and inferiority of the horses probably contributed its quota. A horse over fourteen hands high is a rarity; few have good paces; they have no speed, and are wanting in handiness. Moreover, the majority of them trip violently even at a walk, owing to their thick, heavy shoulders and short, bull-dog necks. Now, equitation, many maintain, is an inherited quality. Generations of riders beget sons with legs long in proportion to their bodies, and so formed as to fit readily to the horse's back, Riders, like poets, are in fact born, seldom made. On the other hand, a nation which never rides, but always walks, will beget sturdy pedestrians. This is the case in Japan, and here a similarity to the Goorka again comes in. It is next to impossible to teach a Goorka to ride; his legs are too short and his thighs too thick. The Japanese as a nation are very long in the body and very short in the leg, a physical conformation dead against good horsemanship.

Allowing for this national disability, the cavalry rode very well; but a glance showed they were not born horsemen. A party of officers from various regiments formed one troop, and were being instructed in troop drill. Their riding was not good, and in most cases the pony was master of the situation. Various parties of recruits were doing riding-school, and some were being taught to jump, the course being a long, straight one, hedged in on both sides. The jumps were small, as they should be for recruits, but not so small as the ludicrous little walls and ditches to be seen in Germany. Two or three squadrons were manœuvring about—and manœuvring very steadily, as long as they trotted. The galloping was not good, and of course very slow. The drill was exactly on the English model, or perhaps one should say German: those systems, however, are practically identical, three or four small troops making up a squadron.

The armament of the cavalry consists of a long carbine, or short rifle, of the Muratta pattern, which is always carried slung on the back; and a slightly curved cut-and-thrust sword, of German make, in a steel scabbard, suspended from the belt by a single sling as in Germany. No sabretaches are worn. The carbine sling is a plain strap, and the carbine is put on and taken off by passing the loop bodily over the head. All the uniforms are rubbed in holes by the friction of the carbine, and the pressure on the back must be severe. A cross-belt supports one pouch, which contains sixteen rounds of ammunition. In war time forty rounds in addition are carried in the holsters. The non-commissioned officers, instead of German swords, wear the national sword, with a modern hilt replacing the two-handed haft of Old Japan. In talking of these old swords to an infantry officer, he assured me that in time of war each officer would cast away his regulation sword and take to the two-handed sword of his ancestors.

A 'battalion' of cavalry consists of three squadrons, each 160 strong. The horses cost on an average about fifty dollars each. Officers' chargers are supplied and fed by the State. A first-class horse will cost as much as 400 dollars. In the school I rode a very handsome little chestnut, fourteen hands, well bred, and very like an Arab. He came from America, and belonged, I believe, to the general. His price was put at 2000 dollars! He would be worth about Rs. 1000 in India, which leaves a margin of about Rs. 3000 a-head profit to any one who cares to send across a batch of Arabs. The rough-riders in this school were long, thin fellows, quite the cut for the business, and dressed like English grooms in their stable gear.

The stables are of wood, commodious and airy, with wooden floors and wooden partitions between the horses. Each horse has a manger and a hay-rack above, as in an English stable. The horse ration consists of four feeds of, at this season (August), beans, bran, and chopped straw mixed, each feed being 1 *sho* or 1½ quarts. At other times whole barley is given. The country horses we noticed live entirely on rice, as in Burmah. The hay is sweet and good, and the feed from 15 lb. to 20 lb. a day. The shoeing is of the usual English pattern.

The saddle is built on the same principle as ours, two side-boards supported by front and back arches. The covering, however, instead of being plain leather, is much padded. It is very fairly comfortable to ride in, but places one rather high off the horse's back. In front are two capacious soft wallets, and on each side, behind the leg, hang large saddle-bags. The greatcoat is carried behind, strapped to the saddle. A plain double bridle without ornaments is used, and a plain breast-strap, but no crupper. The bit is of the ordinary hunting pattern, with a very low port. The stirrup-irons are flat-bottomed and of a peculiar pattern, but hardly large enough. The girths are formed of about a dozen strands of stout whip-cord.

One blanket is carried under the saddle. The trooper wears breeches and boots with spurs, a short coat, and the same cap as the infantry.

I regret much that I can furnish no particulars about the artillery, for, beyond seeing a battery of small guns on the road, I was unfortunate enough to miss the artillery on every occasion. The battery I saw consisted of six small brass guns on miniature carriages, which were drawn by ponies; or the guns could be dismounted and placed on the ponies' backs. There was no artillery officer present who could speak French, and therefore even on this occasion the information gained was more meagre than it might have been. All the ordnance is manufactured in Japan.

Speaking generally of the Japanese army, I think it will be allowed that we have here a very important factor in the politics of the Far East. We have, in fact, some 50,000 excellent troops, who might in more ways than one be of great service to a strong and rich ally like Great Britain. This young army, so speedily and admirably raised, like all young institutions is longing for the day on which it may show its mettle. Any war, against any body, and on any pretext, would be immensely popular with all classes. And if that war chanced to be against China, the Japanese army allied with the British, the national enthusiasm would be unbounded. Pecuniary disability as much as anything prevents this plucky and impetuous little nation from plunging into war with its huge neighbour. Remove that disability—in other words, supply the sinews of war—and we may count on auxiliaries who are well worthy to fight side by side with British troops. Though a British war with China is at this moment a highly improbable contingency, yet the 'Middle Kingdom' in its blind infatuation may any day commit, or allow to be committed, some act the only atonement for which can be war and stern reprisals.

Not only in China, however, but also nearer home, a Japanese army might be of signal service. Between Japan and Siam a well-defined fellow-feeling exists. They are in some sense sister kingdoms, both bent on endeavouring to rise in the comity of nations. Siam, from want of Japanese grit, has failed so far, where the other has succeeded; but still the *camaraderie* remains. Should it at any time become necessary to uphold the integrity of Siam by force of arms, it is not difficult to conjecture on which side the Japanese army and the Japanese fleet will be found arrayed.

Hand-in-glove with the narrower view of what may or may not suit British interests goes the far larger and broader issue, the future of Asia. There is one nation in the world that can make Japan the Great Britain of the Far East, and that nation is the British nation. Sooner or later that huge, unwholesome, semi-barbarous empire of China must succumb before the accumulation of civilisation at her doors. She may fall to Russia, whose land-hunger in Asia is unappeasable; she may fall to England, who is in a chronic and almost comic state of adding new countries to her possessions against her own wishes; with a little timely help she may fall to Japan.

Whilst making these conjectures, it may not be out of place to allude to the immense power wielded by the press, and the immeasurable advantages which might accrue to us by a careful regulation of the British press in Japan. It requires but a few weeks in the country to notice, with regret, the semi-hostile attitude assumed towards the Japanese by the journals, whether American or British, printed in English. If a sailor gets drunk, breaks a rickshaw into pieces, and knocks two front teeth down the coolie's throat, the report in next day's English paper is probably headed, 'Another brutal assault on a sailor.' A ruffian of an American, from the wilds of Texas, draws and shoots a wretched groom, and is, naturally, mobbed in return. In the papers, as likely as not, they gloze over the shooting part, and announce a 'Dastardly attack on an American by an armed crowd.' These are probably the only prints that are ever seen by the people, and the natural impression amongst them undoubtedly must be that Great Britain is a semi-hostile and distinctly brutal country; whereas, as we all know, the most friendly feelings exist throughout our empire for Japan. The purchase of one of the existing journals, or the establishment of a thoroughly friendly daily paper well served with foreign telegrams, would be an investment which, I am convinced, would repay us a hundredfold in the years to come. For a British Minister to impress upon the Mikado's counsellors the friendly feeling of the British nation, in face of the bitter hostility of papers published at his very door, is a task beyond the powers of the most silver-tongued diplomatist.

www.ingramcontent.com/pod-product-compliance
Lightning Source LLC
Chambersburg PA
CBHW032221230426
43666CB00033B/489